SINGAPORE
World City

TUTTLE Publishing

Tokyo | Rutland, Vermont | Singapore

Published by Tuttle Publishing, an imprint of Periplus Editions (HK) Ltd

www.tuttlepublishing.com

ISBN: 978-0-8048-4335-5

Distributed by

North America, Latin America & Europe
Tuttle Publishing
364 Innovation Drive
North Clarendon, VT 05759-9436 U.S.A.
Tel: 1 (802) 773-8930
Fax: 1 (802) 773-6993
info@tuttlepublishing.com
www.tuttlepublishing.com

Japan
Tuttle Publishing
Yaekari Building, 3rd Floor
5-4-12 Osaki
Shinagawa-ku
Tokyo 141-0032
Tel: (81) 3 5437-0171
Fax: (81) 3 5437-0755
sales@tuttle.co.jp
www.tuttle.co.jp

Asia Pacific
Berkeley Books Pte. Ltd.
61 Tai Seng Avenue, #02-12
Singapore 534167
Tel: (65) 6280-1330
Fax: (65) 6280-6290
inquiries@periplus.com.sg
www.periplus.com

Indonesia
PT Java Books Indonesia
Kawasan Industri Pulogadung
JI. Rawa Gelam IV No. 9
Jakarta 13930
Tel: (62) 21 4682-1088
Fax: (62) 21 461-0206
crm@periplus.co.id
www.periplus.com

Printed in Singapore   1311TW

PAGE 1 The outline of the Marina Bay Sands hotel with skypark resembling a giant ship in the sky has become synonymous with the new stylish Singapore. **PAGE 2-3** A colourful light show on the waters of Marina Bay with both new and old skyscrapers of the Financial District behind. **RIGHT** Old and new buildings in midtown illuminated with a fan palm in foreground. **OVERLEAF** View from the Esplanade over the still waters of Marina Bay at dusk.

THE TUTTLE STORY: "BOOKS TO SPAN THE EAST AND WEST"

Many people are surprised to learn that the world's largest publisher of books on Asia had its humble beginnings in the tiny American state of Vermont. The company's founder, Charles Tuttle, came from a New England family steeped in publishing.

Tuttle's father was a noted antiquarian dealer in Rutland, Vermont. Young Charles honed his knowledge of the trade working in the family bookstore, and later in the rare books section of Columbia University Library. His passion for beautiful books—old and new—never wavered throughout his long career as a bookseller and publisher.

After graduating from Harvard, Tuttle enlisted in the military and in 1945 was sent to Tokyo to work on General Douglas MacArthur's staff. He was tasked with helping to revive the Japanese publishing industry, which had been utterly devastated by the war. When his tour of duty was completed, he left the military, married a talented and beautiful singer, Reiko Chiba, and in 1948 began several successful business ventures.

To his astonishment, Tuttle discovered that postwar Tokyo was actually a book-lover's paradise. He befriended dealers in the Kanda district and began supplying rare Japanese editions to American libraries. He also imported American books to sell to the thousands of GIs stationed in Japan. By 1949, Tuttle's business was thriving, and he opened Tokyo's very first English-language bookstore in the Takashimaya Department Store in Ginza, to great success. Two years later, he began publishing books to fulfill the growing interest of foreigners in all things Asian.

Though a westerner, Tuttle was hugely instrumental in bringing a knowledge of Japan and Asia to a world hungry for information about the East. By the time of his death in 1993, he had published over 6,000 books on Asian culture, history and art—a legacy honoured by Emperor Hirohito in 1983 with the "Order of the Sacred Treasure," the highest honour Japan can bestow upon a non-Japanese.

The Tuttle company today maintains an active backlist of some 1,500 titles, many of which have been continuously in print since the 1950s and 1960s—a great testament to Charles Tuttle's skill as a publisher. More than 60 years after its founding, Tuttle Publishing is more active today than at any time in its history, still inspired by Charles Tuttle's core mission—to publish fine books to span the East and West and provide a greater understanding of each.

CONTENTS

PART ONE: **INTRODUCING SINGAPORE**

PART TWO: EXPLORING SINGAPORE

THE LION CITY COMES OF AGE

For people with a limited knowledge of Singapore, it's probably a mere dot of a rock at the southern end of the Malay Peninsula. But, for those in the know, it is so much more: a 700-square kilometre city-state on a tropical island; a teeming metropolis whose powerful skyline is fringed by fecund equatorial vegetation; an intriguing mix of Chinese, Indian, Malay and European inhabitants; few natural resources, but healthy GDP figures and a standard of living that most nations only dream of.

▲ ▲ **PREVIOUS PAGE** Opened in 1870 to commemorate Singapore's crown colony status, the Cavenagh bridge spans the Singapore river in the downtown core.

▲ **ABOVE** Sir Thomas Stamford Raffles (1781–1826) was the founder of modern-day Singapore. His statue by famed sculptor-cum-poet Thomas Woolner stands in front of the Victoria Theatre and Concert Hall. The famous Hainanese chicken rice dish. A rubber stamp for the Republic of Singapore.

▶ **OPPOSITE** The old and the new: Rows of terracotta tiled shophouse roofs in Chinatown are set against a backdrop of skyscrapers in the Financial District.

The story of how Singapore was founded in 1819, prospered under colonial rule, then unburdened itself from its colonial yoke in 1965 and single-handedly transformed its society from third world to first world in less than a couple of decades should be the stuff of legends—except it happens to be true. Certainly Sir Stamford Raffles recognized its potential when he established a British port on what was a largely uninhabited island: he saw it possessed a deep natural harbour, fresh water supplies, plentiful timber for repairing ships, and, being close to the Straits of Malacca, would serve to challenge the Dutch who were dominating the lucrative China to British India trade route at the time.

Over the next few decades, his instincts proved correct. Establishing Singapore as a free port, instigating sensible town planning, and encouraging immigration via low taxation and little restriction resulted in a thriving port city that came to dominate the region. Its status was sealed when it became a Crown Colony on 1 April 1867. Before Raffles arrived there were about 1,000 people—mostly Malays and a few Chinese—living on the island; by 1869, the population had risen to 100,000, consisting mainly of Chinese and Indian immigrants. Their descendents came to form the bulk of the new Singaporeans.

Naturally, this burgeoning population had to be housed, and Raffles' Town Plan—which formed much of the island's early infrastructure—is still in evidence today. Around a colonial core housing financial, administrative and commercial buildings, grew a number of different districts divided into ethnic neighbourhoods, many of which remain. As the colony grew, so did its built environment: plantations were eaten up by residential estates and business premises spread far inland, although large swathes of jungle were left untouched.

The next 100 years of Singapore's development saw more radical change: Even though World War I did not really

affect Singapore, World War II saw the colony capitulate to the Japanese. Between 1942 and 1945, it was occupied by the Japanese Empire, only to emerge afterwards with increasing levels of self-government, a merger with the Federation of Malaya in 1963, and eventual independence two years later. On the morning of the 9th of August 1965, Singapore was established as an independent and sovereign republic.

Since then, a combination of single-minded determination on the part of the government and, more recently, levels of energy and creativity in the nascent Singaporean population have truly transformed the tiny city-state into a global power to be reckoned with. Two bodies—the Economic Development Board and the Housing Development Board—have spearheaded both economic growth and higher standards of living, all the while trying to maintain a balance between cultural and physical heritage and the demands of a growing nation.

Mistakes have been made, the authorities have been accused of high handedness on more than one occasion, and there are always certain grumblings and mumblings to be had. Yet, nobody can deny the fact that Singapore has risen to meet its challenges head on and today stands proud as South East Asia's most livable and most beautiful city.

Recent years have seen a huge makeover of the Central Business District and the creation of a truly eye-catching downtown area at Marina Bay. Old shophouses and colonial buildings are finding new life as fashion-forward galleries, museums and hotels, while glass-and-steel skyscrapers punctuate an already impressive skyline. In line with the government's vision of creating a "City in a Garden", 101 hectares of prime reclaimed land have been transformed into a futuristic public garden (see previous page), aptly showcasing Singapore's ability to transform itself into Asia's premier tropical Garden City.

Today, there's no denying that both the public and private sectors have finally come of age—the city-state is the envy of the region and the world. And, as with all works in progress, while balancing the past with the present, Singapore continues to look towards the future.

▲▲ **PREVIOUS PAGE** The Supertree Grove at Gardens by the Bay rises from a sea of green below. Ranging in height from 25 to 50 metres, they provide shade and work as environmental engines for the gardens.

▲ **ABOVE** Transport and trade: A 1980s photograph of the Singapore river showing hundreds of bumboats moored at Boat Quay on right.

◀ **OPPOSITE PAGE: CLOCKWISE FROM TOP LEFT** View of the Fullerton Hotel, housed in the old General Post Office building (1924–28), framed through the Anderson bridge (1910).

◀ Five blocks of restored warehouses on the Singapore river house the various restaurants and nightclubs of Clarke Quay. Two moored Chinese junks (*tongkangs*) have been refurbished into floating pubs and restaurants.

◀ Double Happiness lanterns hang in front of colourful shophouse shutters.

◀ Detail from the *gopuram* or entrance tower of the Sri Mariamman temple featuring elaborate plaster sculptures.

◀ The Financial District's gleaming towers form the backdrop to this photo of the Singapore river with the Elgin bridge (1929) in the foreground. Named after Lord Elgin, Governor-General of India (21 March 1862 to 20 November 1863), it was the first vehicular bridge to cross the river.

THE BUSINESS OF GOVERNMENT

Despite its tiny size and limited resources, since Independence in 1965 Singapore has developed into a highly successful economy with one of the highest per-capita GDPs in the world. Undoubtedly this has been in large part because of extensive government planning and intervention, initially under the leadership of Lee Kuan Yew, then his deputy Goh Chok Tong and more recently under Lee's eldest son Lee Hsien Loong. All three have been or are leaders of the People's Action Party (PAP), Singapore's premier political party.

▲ **TOP** A dignified sign outside Singapore's new Parliament building. The red-and-white national flag features a white crescent moon facing a pentagon of five small white five-pointed stars. Gleaming office towers in the Financial District.

▶ **OPPOSITE** Skyscrapers in the Financial District. In 2008, the government announced plans to add 85 hectares of offices in the Marina Bay area; on completion it will be more than twice the size of London's Canary Wharf.

Since the early days after independence from British rule, the Singapore government has combined Economic Development Board planning with free-market policies all the while attracting foreign investment. For example, the country's sovereign wealth fund Temasek Holdings is a major investor in some of Singapore's largest companies, such as Singapore Airlines, SingTel and MediaCorp, yet many other smaller companies have been encouraged to thrive in what is effectively a free-market economy. This middle way between government control and swashbuckling entrepreneurialism termed the "Singapore Model" has been much lauded by economists as a viable route towards stability and growth.

Singapore's traditional portfolio of shipping, petro-chemical, electronic and chemical industries is supported by its strategic port which allows it to purchase raw materials such as oil, gas and water and refine them for re-export. Since 2010, its two casinos have substantially added to the country's revenues, allowing Singapore to buy natural resources and goods that it does not have or does not manufacture. Furthermore, always looking to the future, the government has more recently embarked on investments in biotechnology, financial services, the opening and running of higher education institutions, and medical tourism.

The "Singapore Model" with its Confucian ideals that value traditional hierarchies and social order above individual hopes and desires has produced a diligent population that has, for the most part, benefitted from this social and economic stability. Most have high levels of savings in the government's mandatory Central Provident Fund that is both a money maker and a source of funds for the population's healthcare

LEE KUAN YEW:
SINGAPORE'S FOUNDING FATHER

No book on Singapore would be complete without more than one mention of Lee Kuan Yew, Singapore's first prime minister and the man credited with directing the country from Independence to developed nation status. Born on 16 September 1923 as a third-generation Straits-born Chinese, Lee excelled early, winning a scholarship to Cambridge University and graduating with a first class honours degree in law in 1949.

In 1954 Lee helped co-found the People's Action Party (PAP), shrewdly representing its more moderate faction, all the while negotiating to extract Singapore from its colonial masters, then later vying for power within the Federation of Malaya. After Independence, he became the Republic of Singapore's first prime minister, a post he retained for 31 years.

Whatever one may think of his autocratic style, Lee should be credited in large part for transforming Singapore from a tiny third-world island with a disparate and unruly population into a shining model of efficiency and prosperity. It was his personal vision that guided this extraordinary journey: early infrastructure projects, the attraction of foreign investment, rapid industrialization and the development of an English-language education system all garnered quick results. These were further consolidated with more infrastructure, defense, health, education, pension and housing schemes, as well as urban regeneration programmes and home-ownership plans.

After resigning in 1990, Lee has held two advisory roles, first as Senior Minister, then as Minister Mentor: Frequently sought after for opinions and guidance, despite frail health, he remains very much involved in government policy.

and retirement needs. Interestingly enough, the CPF was initiated in 1955 by the colonial government, but was continued after independence.

In recent years, as the population has grown and expanded, the PAP has faced some criticism for its rigid, paternalistic style despite the fact that Singapore is a stable, pro-business, relatively corruption-free city-state. Some argue that the government is too focused on economic growth and has hindered individuality, artistic prowess and personal freedoms. In response to this, there has been a gradual loosening of this control, with the PAP turning its attention to its education system and the arts, entertainment and tourism sectors, all the while still continuing to bolster the economy. As a result, Singapore seems more relaxed than it was a couple of decades ago: Art, architecture and design, for example, are thriving as never before.

This does not mean to say that the country has changed direction. There is still little political opposition, a type of self-censorship exists within the press, and the government has broad powers to limit citizens' rights. For example, the Public Order Act of 2009 prohibits outdoor public processions or assemblies without police permits. Nevertheless, even as some parts of the population become ever more vocal as the nation matures, the majority continue to be incredibly hard-working, with many putting in long hours in the office all the while valuing family and tradition above all.

Certainly, when one compares standards of living in Singapore with those of its neighbours, the country scores highly. Crime is low, stability is high, and the population is friendly, well-educated and secure. This, no doubt, is due in large part to government policies, as well as to Singaporeans' hard work and commitment to law and order.

◀ **OPPOSITE TOP** Singapore's President Yushof bin Ishak receives the salute during the ceremonial march along the *padang* on the occasion of Singapore's first Independence day celebration on 9 August 1966.

SINGAPORE'S PARLIAMENT

As with many former British colonies, Singapore adopted Britain's Westminster parliamentary model upon Independence. The country is a democratic republic with the President of Singapore being the head of state, the Prime Minister of Singapore being the head of government, and executive power exercised by the cabinet. The parliament consists of a single chamber, currently composed of 87 elected seats.

Even though Singapore is supposed to be a multi-party state, the People's Action Party (PAP) has won every general election since independence. Its actions in suppressing opposition, especially in the first two decades after Independence, have led many (both within and without the country) to argue that Singapore is a *de-facto* one-party state. Be that as it may, the system operates with a governing party and an opposition (which usually wins two to four seats).

Firstly housed in a dignified Victorian building that was originally a merchant's private home (now an arts centre known as Old Parliament House), the government moved round the corner to New Parliament House in 1999. Designed and built by architects from the former Public Works Department, it sports three new buildings with a sober, grey-toned colonnaded façade and one restored colonial building. Situated adjacent the Singapore river, it blends harmoniously with the civic quarter architecture that surrounds it.

A MULTI-ETHNIC, MULTI-CULTURAL RAINBOW

Sitting in a physiotherapist's waiting room a few years ago, I was intrigued by a conversation between a client and the receptionist. The latter, sporting a nametag, was being quizzed by the client as to which part of Sri Lanka she came from. "I am not Sri Lankan," came the reply, "I am Singaporean." Undaunted, the client continued, "But your name … it is a Sri Lankan name." "Regardless, I am Singaporean," came the reply.

This line of questioning went back and forth a few more times, with the client adamant she was of Sri Lankan origin and the receptionist sticking to her story: whatever her name, she was a Singaporean— and proud of it. At no point did she concede that her parents or grandparents or great-grandparents had emigrated from Sri Lanka, nor that she had South Asian roots. As far as she was concerned, she was from Singapore.

▲ **TOP** From left to right: The Chinese, Indians and Malays comprise the majority of Singapore's multi-ethnic population.

◄ **OPPOSITE** The country's National Day is celebrated each year on 9th August, in commemoration of Singapore's independence from Malaysia in 1965. Typically there is a parade, a fireworks display and more. Here flag-waving schoolchildren, dressed in patriotic red and white, show support for their country.

It's a telling encounter, because it encapsulates much about the average Singaporean: he or she is an immigrant or comes from immigrant stock; her ethnicity may be different to her neighbour's; he could be a Christian, she an agnostic; his skin colour, his background, his family … all may be the opposite of his wife's. Yet, where they are all united is in their nationality.

Certainly, in the early days of colonization, an abundance of merchants and migrants were attracted to the new outpost as business and commerce flourished. Most came from the southern provinces of China, Indonesia, the Indian subcontinent and the Middle East—all looking for the prospect of a better life. Many would have intended returning to their native countries, but life, wealth, new roots and inter-marriage resulted in a large proportion of them remaining. Today's population, descended from this early mix, is a melting pot of complementary ethnic groups, roughly consisting of 77 percent Chinese, 14 percent Malay, 8 percent Indians and 1 percent Eurasians, plus a sprinkling of people of other descent.

As such, Singapore makes for an exciting multi-racial, multi-religious, multi-ethnic mix. At school, every child is required to repeat the National Pledge daily: "We, the citizens of Singapore, pledge ourselves as one united people, regardless of race, language or religion, to build a democratic society based on justice and equality so as to achieve happiness, prosperity and progress for our nation." Written shortly after the nation's independence by one of the pioneer leaders of independent Singapore, Sinnathamby Rajaratnam, who saw language, race and religion as divisive factors, it emphasized that these differences can be overcome if Singaporeans care enough about their country.

There's no doubt that this attitude has been embraced by the populace at large: Singapore is a rare example of a multi-cultural society with remarkable tolerance for racial and religious differences. As one leader noted: "One is first and foremost a Singaporean, then a Chinese, Malay, Indian, or other."

A GREAT LEAP FORWARD IN MUSIC, THEATRE, DANCE AND THE VISUAL ARTS

Recent investment in the Arts in the form of new galleries, venues and arts-related events has seen a huge leap forward in Singapore's arts scene. On any given day or night, there is always something new to watch, listen to, or visit. Be it a concert in the stunning double-domed Esplanade or colonial Victoria Concert Hall, a historical talk at the National Archives, a rock concert in one of the city parks, or a specialist arts fair, the events calendar is action-packed. Both local and foreign attractions proliferate throughout the year.

▲ **TOP** The futuristic outline of the Moshe Safdie designed ArtScience Museum on Marina Bay. Durian dome at the Esplanade complex. The white facade of the neo-Classical National Museum with Corinthian columns.

▶ **OPPOSITE TOP** The rotunda dome at the National Museum is fitted with stained glass panels that were fully restored in 2005.

▶ **OPPOSITE BOTTOM** "The Dancing Sky", a stunning show of aerial acrobatics, dance, light and music by Italian company Studio Festi, at the National Museum's Night Festival, an event held on the 18th July 2008. The facade of the neo-Classical National Museum is seen in the background.

The National Arts Council, charged with overseeing art appreciation in Singapore, organizes free concerts in lush park surrounds year round, while other annual fixtures include the Singapore Arts Fair (four weeks in May and June), running the gamut from theatre through dance and film to concerts, and the Fringe Festival in January that concentrates on theatre, dance and the visual arts. Two annual art fairs—Art Stage and the Affordable Art Fair—attract crowds, while other annual events include the world music festival WOMAD, Ballet under the Stars, the International Comedy Festival and more.

On any given night, you can easily choose from a wide variety of genres—Chinese opera, Indian dance, Western stand-up comedy, a world-class Shakespeare production, for example. Theatre is particularly strong, with a plethora of local companies staging productions, often by local playwrights with surprising social commentary, complemented by large Western touring musicals and shows. Of particular note is the W!LD RICE company that creates what it calls "glocal" works inspired by both Singaporean society and universal issues and the Singapore Repertory Theatre, more associated with Broadway-style productions. Dance is represented by over 30 dance companies and societies, with the Singapore Dance Theatre staging about 28 performances each year, and a number of smaller companies specializing in ethnic dance—South East Asian, Indian and the like. Classical music is represented by the superb Singapore Symphony Orchestra; set up in 1979, it plays about 100 concerts at the Esplanade annually.

Art and architecture is indelibly linked, as evidenced by the intriguing mix of public sculptures found along the river, the world-class Esplanade complex with its durian domes, and the many colonial buildings that have found new life as venues for the arts. The Arts House at the Old Parliament is a particular case in point, as is the Singapore Art Museum (SAM)

housed in a graceful 19th-century former school building. Similarly, many museums—in former classical civic buildings, Chinese shophouses or old fortifications—showcase not only exhibits relating to Singapore and South East Asia, but the actual architecture and interiors themselves.

Cases in point include the Asian Civilisations Museum, the Peranakan Museum, the Baba House and the Chinatown Heritage Centre: each offers more than an adequate glimpse of a particularly Singaporean experience as well as South East Asian and Asian artifacts and culture. Local and other history is on display at the "people's museum" or the National Museum of Singapore, while experiences of Singaporeans during World War II are adeptly recreated at Fort Siloso, the Memories at Old Ford Factory sited in the building where the British army surrendered to Japanese forces and Reflections at Bukit Chandu, housed in a restored black-and-white colonial bungalow amidst the lush surrounds of Bukit Chandu (Opium Hill), close to where the legendary Battle of Pasir Panjang was fought. High on atmosphere, and often high-tech as well, there is much to be learned and enjoyed at these venues.

◀ **OPPOSITE: CLOCKWISE FROM TOP LEFT** The Asian Civilisations Museum, located at historic Empress Place, was opened on 1st March 2003. The museum presents the history and culture of Singapore's ancestral cultures.

◀ A dance performance on the lawn of the Asian Civilisations Museum opens the Singapore River Festival, a week-long programme of performances and parades in the quays along the Singapore river.

◀ The ArtScience Museum, built in the shape of a lotus, features changing exhibitions that often rely on technology as a medium for their message.

◀ One of the performers at the 2008 "The Dancing Sky" performance at the National Museum.

◀ An intimate outdoor stage at Esplanade—Theatres by the Bay hosts an evening concert.

◀ The stunning blue facade of the Baba House, a traditional Peranakan pre-war terrace house turned museum. Formerly owned by shipping tycoon, Wee Bin, it was probably built in the 1860s. Today, it is owned and managed by Wee Lin, a sixth-generation descendent of Wee Bin, and contains furniture, mementoes and memories of a typical wealthy Peranakan household.

▲ **TOP** A colourful poster for a W!LD RICE production—an imaginative local spin on the world's favourite fairytale.

SINGAPORE CINEMA

Some argue that Singapore's film-making heyday occurred during the 1950s and '60s, but in the last decade homegrown cinema has experienced a renaissance of sorts with offerings that are considerably more profound and professional than Singapore's television industry. Local directors such as Eric Khoo, Jack Neo, Royston Tan, Kelvin Tong and Anthony Chen represent a younger generation that is making waves both internationally in film festivals and in cinemas at home.

Khoo's *12 Storeys*, *Mee Pok Man* and *Be with Me* are accurate portrayals of Singaporean life in its "heartlands", while Jack Neo is well known for commercially successful satirical works, such as *I Not Stupid* and *I Not Stupid Too*. More recently, in May 2013, film-maker Anthony Chen became the first Singaporean to win the prestigious Camera d'Or prize for "Best First Feature Film" at the Cannes Film Festival. His movie, *Ilo Ilo*, tells a domestic story of a family and their new maid.

Whether visitors can catch any of these movies while they are in Singapore really depends on luck and timing, but April sees the Singapore International Film Festival, a month-long event that was launched in 1987. In addition to a varied itinerary of international and local films, there are seminars, work-shops and exhibitions on film-making. It is also worth checking local listings for other 2-week film festivals of European cinema—Italian, French and so on.

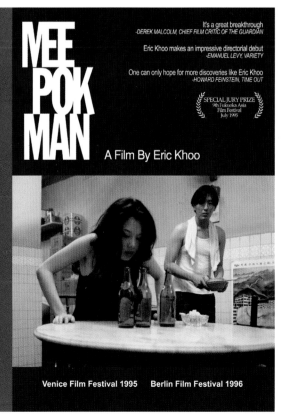

It's a great breakthrough
-DEREK MALCOLM, CHIEF FILM CRITIC OF THE GUARDIAN

Eric Khoo makes an impressive directorial debut
-EMANUEL LEVY, VARIETY

One can only hope for more discoveries like Eric Khoo
-HOWARD FEINSTEIN, TIME OUT

SPECIAL JURY PRIZE
9th Fukuoka Asia
Film Festival
July 1995

MEE POK MAN

A Film By Eric Khoo

Venice Film Festival 1995   Berlin Film Festival 1996

THE NATIONAL OBSESSION

In the same manner that the English obsess about the weather, Singaporeans obsess about food. They are extremely knowledgeable and critical about their various food options— and even greet each other with the phrase "Have you taken your lunch yet?" as opposed to "Good day" or "Good morning". As is to be expected, every imaginable dish within every imaginable price range is available in a variety of eateries around the island.

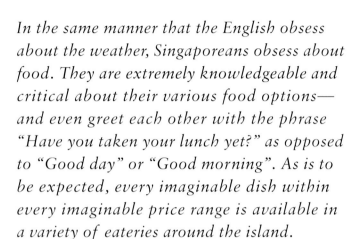

▲ **TOP** Dishes from all corners of the globe: Chicken satay on wooden skewers. Thick noodles with prawn. Laksa, a spicy noodle dish. Sushi. Hamburger. Egg fried rice.

▶ **OPPOSITE** Even though the Geylang area is mainly known for its brothels and girlie bars, it also has a glorious food culture. One of the oldest Malay enclaves in Singapore, its *lorongs* or small side streets are home to numerous eateries, coffee shops and makeshift stalls. It also has a lively "old Singapore" atmosphere.

Singapore's history is to be found in its hawker centres and food courts, unpretentious eating areas where a variety of stall owners cook and sell fresh food on the spot. Every single type of multi-ethnic cuisine is available in these establishments with individual stallholders often third or fourth generation family businesses. Large plastic tables and chairs occupy the centre of the space, while a variety of kitchens ring the perimeter. Hawker centres tend to be semi outdoor; food centres will be in the basement of shopping centres. You base your party at a table, then wander at will ordering a selection of dishes that are cooked fresh and brought to your table. High standards of hygiene, uniformly excellent food, and very reasonable prices are the hallmark of these traditional eating centres.

Another traditional eatery is the *kopitiam* or coffee shop taken from the Hokkien word *tiam* that translates as "shop". Typically family-run, you're likely to find marble-topped tables, bentwood chairs and a bustling atmosphere in these shopfront affairs. Manned by an "auntie" or an "uncle" and also usually family run, they are one of the mainstays of Singaporean dining.

In addition to these popular joints, there are any number of restaurants, both indoor and outdoor, selling every possible cuisine and suiting every pocket. As is to be expected, local specialties include a variety of Chinese cuisines, north and south Indian dishes, Malay and Indonesian staples, and the unique flavours of Peranakan or Straits Chinese home cooking. In addition, there is any number of other South East Asian restaurants—Laos noodle joints, Vietnamese and Thai restaurants, Korean barbecues, Japanese *kaiseki* and sushi— even places that specialize in the cuisines of Cambodia and Myanmar. Furthermore, international and fusion fare is represented by a seemingly endless number of chefs who have set up restaurants serving French, Italian, Greek, Australian, Californian dishes, and more.

The high-end gourmet scene is thriving, especially in the top five-star hotels, and Singapore is known for its World Gourmet Summit and International Food Festival when visiting chefs cook up a storm with accompanying fine wines and cognacs. But for a more local flavour, nothing beats hawker-style Chinese, Indian, Malay and Peranakan dishes and some of the homegrown specialties such as chilli crab and fish head curry.

South Indian cuisine is well represented in Singapore as many early immigrants were Tamils: super-spicy curries, often utilizing coconut milk and flavoured with mint, curry and coriander leaves, are a particular favourite served on banana leaves in numerous inexpensive restaurants in the Little India area. That's not to say that north Indian *tandoor* cuisine, as well as Indian Muslim food isn't popular: *roti prata* (derived from the word *paratha*) is a crispy-crunchy type of pancake served with curry often as a late-night, post-clubbing snack, while a number of different *biriyani* or saffron-scented rice dishes are also well liked.

On the Chinese front, there are literally too many authentic cuisines to mention: Be it Szechuan, Cantonese, Teochew or Hakka, Chinese chefs are very inventive, with many adapting their dishes to local tastes and ingredients. Some of the best loved are seafood dishes like chilli crab, arguably Singapore's national dish, with crispy duck hot on its heels! Fried spring rolls or *popiah* make for a tasty snack, while staple noodle or *mee* dishes, *won ton* dumplings and Hainanese chicken rice, steamed and served with a clear chicken stock, are all firm favourites amongst Singaporeans.

Peranakan women, called *Nyonya*, are famed in Malaysia, Indonesia and Singapore for their home cooking which is an expressive medley of eclecticism. In *Nyonya* dishes, we see the Malay fondness for chillies, *belacan* (dried shrimp paste) and coconut flesh and milk incorporated into traditional Chinese recipes. Pungent, spicy and fragrant, cooks say it is all in the preparation—which can literally take hours. Extended periods of marination, all spices pounded fresh, only the freshest of local ingredients and the best cuts—all contribute to this delightfully distinctive cuisine.

Finally, we cannot finish a description of food without mentioning the importance of Malay cuisine. Essentially a mixture of peninsular Malaysia dishes with influences from the Indonesian islands, most dishes are served with rice. *Satay*, small bamboo skewers with chunks of chicken, mutton or beef, marinated then grilled over charcoal and dipped in a spicy peanut sauce finds its way into many kitchens. Or try *nasi goreng*, a fried rice dish that is really as much Chinese as Malay; it's a good example of the multi-national flavour of Singaporean cuisine.

▲ **ABOVE** Singapore lends itself to casual outdoor dining, and nowhere is this more apparent than along the Singapore river. Here, a row of pubs, eateries, and even a microbrewery line the river at Riverside Point.

◄ **OPPOSITE: CLOCKWISE FROM TOP LEFT** Hainanese chicken rice set with a side dish of baby *kailan*, a crunchy local vegetable.

◄ A richly ornate lantern hangs above a table setting at the True Blue restaurant, a Peranakan establishment adjacent the Peranakan museum. Decor, food and displays form a good introduction to this unique culture.

◄ A variety of different *satay* grilled over charcoal and served with peanut sauce and fresh cucumber and onion slices.

◄ Chilli crab is much loved by Singaporeans: usually mud crabs are chosen and stir-fried in a semi-thick, sweet and savoury tomato and chilli based sauce.

◄ *Zongzi* or sticky rice dumplings are made from glutinous rice stuffed with different fillings and wrapped in bamboo, reed, or other flat leaves. Steamed or boiled, they are often eaten during the Dragon Boat Festival.

◄ An atmospheric, lively pub and restaurant in Emerald Hill, an area of conserved shophouses off Orchard Road.

THE OTHER NATIONAL OBSESSION

When people talk about shopping they invariably mention "Orchard", as Singapore's equivalent of Fifth Avenue in New York or Oxford Street in London is known. A 1.5 km one-way street lined with malls, hotels and offices, Orchard Road contains every brand one can think of—and more. However, don't be fooled into thinking this is your only option: Singapore has plenty of other retail therapy on offer.

▲ **TOP** A poster advertising Singapore's annual Fashion Festival. Humour in a roadside sign on Orchard Road. Jutting out over the waters of Marina Bay is the Moshi Safdie designed futuristic glass-and-steel pavilion that houses one of only 12 Louis Vuitton Island Maison stores found worldwide.

▶ **OPPOSITE** An exterior view of ION Orchard captures the curvy structure of this landmark shopping mall designed by British architects Benoy in 2009.

▶▶ **OVERLEAF** A sculptural Chinese New Year decoration graces Orchard Road in front of the up market Paragon shopping mall. The theme in 2012 for the decorations was "Colourful & Brilliant".

Even though you aren't likely to bag a bargain, unless you shop during late May to early July when the Great Singapore Sale is on, what you will find in Singapore is a huge choice of goods and a very convenient shopping experience. It is easy to get from mall to mall, quality is high and prices are fixed, so you don't have to worry about getting ripped off. But if the mall isn't for you, there are steamy bazaars, outdoor wet markets (for fruit, veg, fish and meat, as well as sundry other goods), small neighbourhood shops usually on the ground floor of shophouses, and a few well-established department stores. Singaporeans seem to obsess about shopping almost as obsessively as they obsess about food—so there is something for everybody in pretty much every category.

Diversity is also to be found in the goods on offer: From international brand names to quirky local and Asian labels, fashion is well represented. Singapore is keen to be seen as the region's fashion capital with its annual Singapore Fashion Festival in April unveiling collections from international powerhouses and talented Asian designers alike. Along with the parties and press releases, there are runway shows and fashion exhibitions as well. For the most part, Orchard is your best bet for Western clothes, whilst regional attire may be found elsewhere: saris in Little India and sarong and *kebaya* in Chinatown and the Arab Quarter, for example.

These areas are also good for a more local shopping experience. Chinese silks, traditional Chinese medicines and herbs, Asian antiques and crafts, made-in-China souvenirs, and more are all to be found in the grid of lanes off South Bridge Road in Chinatown. For sure, there's a lot of tourist tat, but the atmosphere in this buzzy area of low-rise shophouses is an attraction in itself. Similarly, the Arab Quarter is worth a wander: set around the Sultan Mosque are a number of small

lanes of shophouses carrying a good selection of fabrics ranging from Indonesian and Malaysian batiks to Chinese silks and Indian cottons, as well as handmade perfume bottles and basket wares. And if it is Indian wares you are after—saris, incense, gold jewellery, henna tattoos and the like—the alleyways and shops around Serangoon Road won't disappoint. This is also the location of Mustafa: open 24 hours a day, this venerable institution stocks an eclectic collection of goods from Bollywood DVDs to white goods, fresh food, luggage and electronics.

Even though the latter aren't as cheap as they used to be, there are a few malls that deal exclusively in electronic goods, from cameras to computers and an assortment of accessories. Here, you can do a bit of bargaining and it pays to do some research before you arrive: many of the shopkeepers have a great sales patter. The same can be said for the carpet sellers: a number of carpet dealers have made Singapore their home over the generations and they stock an extensive selection of Middle Eastern and Asian carpets and rugs. But, remember, they are true professionals; before you know it, you'll be organizing a shipment of rugs that you didn't need or particularly want!

With all antiques, it is sensible to get a certificate of authenticity and a proper receipt. The same can be said for artworks, which are now one of Singapore's hottest exports. Along with ARTSingapore, Art Stage Singapore and the Affordable Art Fair all plying Asian and other talent, there are literally hundreds of art galleries, showcasing an amazing variety of artists, genres and prices. Again, it helps to do your homework before you purchase.

Finally, mention must be made of flea markets … the true antithesis of the air-conditioned mall. The oldest and best-loved is the Sungei Road Thieves' Market—four roads of kerbside stalls with old men selling anything from chipped crockery to old currency, broken radios to used clothing. The market takes its name from its 1930s' heyday when it was a mecca for stolen goods; today, the stuff is bona fide, but whether you actually want to purchase any of it is another matter. Collectors would be better off at the Clarke Quay sunday market or the Temple Street bazaar: both have stalls selling old memorabilia from China and Singapore, including Chairman Mao mementoes, antique bronze wares, hand-embroidered bead handbags and the like. Again, the atmosphere is part of the attraction at both these bustling venues.

▲ **TOP** South East Asian art on display at Aryaseni Art Gallery.

▲ **ABOVE** Antique religious statuary, such as Buddhas, Taoist deities, monk statues and more are easily available at specialist art and antique shops in Singapore.

◄ **OPPOSITE: CLOCKWISE FROM TOP LEFT** Modern art is readily available in Singapore, both at galleries and specialist art fairs.

◄ An indie fashion store on trendy Haji Lane in the Arab Quarter.

◄ Chinese porcelain pieces in a high-end antiques gallery.

◄ A catwalk show of designs from Priyadarshini Rao at the annual Singapore Fashion Festival.

◄ A row of select shops lines the mall at Resorts World Sentosa.

◄ A selection of rare and authentic Khmer, Thai, Burmese and Chinese sculptures and Chinese ceramics from Asia Ancient Gallery.

◄ All the high-end, international brands, including Prada, line the malls on Orchard.

ASIA'S PREMIER GARDEN CITY

Surprisingly, about half of Singapore's 700 square kilometres of land is reserved for parks, reservoirs, a few small farms, military training grounds and some remaining areas of untouched primary forest. For such a built-up conurbation, it is encouraging that there is so much green.

Being just north of the equator, Singapore is hot, wet, and steamy pretty much year round. As such, it contains an enormous variety of flora—in fact, Dr David Bellamy, a renowned English botanist, once estimated that Singapore contained more plant species than are found in the whole of North America! The island used to be totally covered with dense lowland tropical rain forest, with mangroves along the coasts and tidal creeks and freshwater swamp forests in its interior. As settlement increased from the 1840s onwards, much of the forest was cut down to make way for nutmeg, gambier, clove, pepper and cocoa plantations. As a result, many plant species, including 60 species of mangrove orchids, disappeared—and great tracts of jungle were cleared.

Thankfully, at the turn of the century, forest reserves were set up and, today, the National Parks Board protects about 3,000 hectares of natural reserves. These include the Bukit Timah Nature Reserve, the Sungei Buloh Wetland Reserve, the Labrador Nature Reserve, as well as the Central Catchment Nature Reserve that contains most of the country's fresh water.

▲ **TOP** The tiger may be extinct, but Singapore is home to a rich selection of animal and bird life: Large monitor lizard, stork (three species are resident in Singapore), green tree snake, long-tailed macaque.

▶ **OPPOSITE** A serene view of one of the disused granite quarries on rural Pulau Ubin that has been cleverly transformed into a picturesque lake and now attracts a wide variety of bio-diversity.

These areas are home to more than 840 flowering plants and over 500 species of animals—including towering tropical trees, palms, rattans, ferns, orchids, gingers and many more. In addition, rich bio-diversity is to be found in a multitude of parks and gardens, in plantings along many highways and roads, in collections of heritage trees, and along an extensive network of "park connectors". These comprise cycling, rollerblading, jogging and walking tracks that link certain parks within the city.

As a result, Singapore justifiably markets itself as Asia's "Garden City". With strong conservation policies and active promotion of green recreation, it seeks to promote its natural resources for residents and tourists alike. Few urban areas contain so many pockets of green—from tiny city parks and park connectors to the massive Botanic Gardens and various nature reserves. In addition, there is on-going research and development into urban bio-diversity on a wider scale.

Visitors should not miss the world-famous Botanic Gardens and the newer Gardens by the Bay, not to mention a trip to the nearby island of Pulau Ubin or a hike in the Bukit Timah Nature Reserve. The latter is home to numerous long-tailed macaques, monitor lizards, squirrels, as well as a wide variety of snakes, while wild boar are abundant on Ubin. Orchid lovers will not be disappointed by a trip to the Mandai Orchid Garden or the National Orchid Gardens within the Botanic Gardens, while birders are advised to head to the Sungei Buloh Wetland Reserve, a major stopover for migratory birds, that also contains otters, monitor lizards and a few saltwater crocodiles. In addition, many man-made attractions, such as the zoo, Jurong Bird Park and East Coast Park are veritable oases of green in themselves—it isn't a coincidence that the zoo's true name is the Singapore Zoological Gardens.

THE NATIONAL PARKS BOARD

Responsible for providing and enhancing the greenery in Singapore, NParks (as the organization is known) manages Singapore's four nature reserves and over 300 parks. It is also the impetus behind the extensive streetscape plantings and the grid of park connectors that display a huge variety of flowering tropical plants. In addition, it actively engages the community in its green infrastructure projects, with the aim of improving residents' lifestyles.

NParks' history is closely intertwined with the history of tree planting in Singapore. This began with Lee Kuan Yew's vision to create a city-state within a garden environment consisting of parks, gardens and open spaces linked by a matrix of tree-lined roads and park connectors. He believed that not only would such an environment benefit its inhabitants, it would attract foreign investors to the country. The specialist Parks and Trees Unit that oversaw this work was the forerunner of the National Parks Board (which was eventually formed in 1996).

The Mission Statement of NParks—"to create the best living environment through excellent greenery and recreation, in partnership with the community" —sums up its overall aim, but doesn't really do justice to the hordes of gardeners, horticulturalists, educators and more that passionately tend to the city-state's green areas. Without them, Singapore would be a very different city indeed.

◄ **OPPOSITE: CLOCKWISE FROM TOP LEFT** A flight of steps along one of the many peaceful paths that traverse through the Bukit Timah Nature Reserve. As this forest was never extensively cleared for cultivation, it is home to a vast variety of plants. In fact, Alfred Russel Wallace declared it to be "exceedingly productive".

◄ Designed to evoke inner peace and meditation, the Japanese Garden in Jurong contains many elements from traditional Japanese garden design—arched bridges, stone lanterns, rest houses, ponds and gravel chip paved areas.

◄ A stand of *nibong* palm trees graces the shore of one of the lakes in the Botanic Gardens. Founded in 1859, it has recently been suggested that the gardens deserve UNESCO World Heritage status.

◄ The Botanic Gardens has 6.2 hectares of one of the oldest remnants of primary rainforest in Singapore. Only a few minutes' walk from the downtown area, it is home to 314 species of flora. There are three layers of trees—the emergents (45 m), the canopy tree layer (35 m) and the lower tree layer (25 m)—as well as an understorey, all full of rich plant life. A walk here is truly a jungle walk.

FROM COLONIAL TO POST-MODERN:
A FASCINATING POLYGLOT OF STYLES

Unlike many other Asian cities that have buried all reminders of their colonial past, Singapore has managed to retain plenty in the way of architectural heritage dating back to the British era. Certainly, great swathes of old buildings were destroyed during the 1950s and '60s when Singapore was racing towards modernity, but luckily the brakes were applied before it was too late. Today, much of Chinatown, the Arab Quarter and Little India remain intact with beautifully restored shophouses, there is plenty in the way of extant colonial architecture in the civic centre, and recent years have seen the rise of some impressive modern buildings.

▲ **TOP** A short stroll round Singapore allows visitors access to innumerable architectural styles: A drawing of the elevation of the old Supreme Court building, currently being transformed into an arts centre; the new Supreme Court designed by the British architect Sir Norman Foster in 2005 with its distinctly contemporary flying saucer shape; shophouse facades in the Joo Chiat area.

▶ **OPPOSITE** View looking up towards a skylight from the civic plaza at the eco-friendly National Library building. The wind tunnel design keeps the area cool as heat is drawn upwards and dissipated by the giant fin like structures (top left).

Most tourists will start their exploration of Singapore in the downtown area that comprises the colonial core with the *padang* or cricket pitch at its centre and the Singapore river running alongside. Much of pioneer colonial architect George D Coleman's work is featured here: along with planning, surveying and overseeing Singapore's early townscape, he designed many of its notable civic buildings—the Armenian church, Caldwell House in CHIJMES and Old Parliament House with their Palladian-adapted-to-the-Tropics style enduring to this day. Other mid 19th-century buildings of note include St Andrew's Cathedral and the Cathedral of the Good Shepherd, while the 1930s' Old Supreme Court (currently undergoing transformation into an arts and cultural centre) still stands proud as the last structure in the style of Classic architecture to be built before Independence.

In recent years, this downtown area has benefited greatly from the addition of some modern edifices that have become synonymous with 21st-century Singapore: The Esplanade concert hall and theatre complex, the Marina Bay Sands in adjacent Marina Bay, Norman Foster's Supreme Court, I M Pei's glass-and-steel Gateway towers, and the eco-friendly National Library are all cases in point. All are within walking distance of the old colonial core—as is the Central Business District with its rather more functional high-rise office towers.

For a more Asian flavour, one needs to stroll west to Chinatown or east to the Arab Quarter (Kampong Glam) or Little India. Here, row upon row of archetypal Singapore shophouses delight the eye with their lively facades and colourful pastel hues. Long and thin, with a shop on the ground floor and living quarters above, the shophouse traces its roots back to mainland Chinese architecture; it was introduced to the region by Chinese merchants, so there are many similar buildings in Malacca and other ancient city ports along the shores of maritime South East Asia. In Raffles' 1822 Ordinances outlining the fledgling settlement's town plan, he determined that each house "should have a verandah of a certain depth, open at all times as a continued and covered

passage on each side of the street". This takes the form of the continuous covered walkway in front of each row of shophouses that allows pedestrians to walk freely protected from both tropical sun and rains.

These—and multiple styles of shophouse that developed in later decades—remain as a testament to both Raffles and the practicalities of the architectural typology. Many still contain shops on the ground floor, although others have been converted into bars, restaurants and gallery or office spaces. Of particular note are the Chinatown Heritage Centre and the Baba House in Chinatown: the former has exhibits and "rooms" showcasing how these buildings were divided into dozens of miniscule, dark cubicles to house scores of the settlement's early migrants, while the latter has been reconstructed and refurbished to show how life was lived by a wealthy Peranakan family during the first half of the 20th century.

Even though Singapore is keen to promote both its shophouse and colonial architecture, it should be stressed that the majority of Singaporeans live in high-rise apartment blocks built by the Housing Development Board (HDB) in what are called the heartlands—satellite towns for the masses. HDB developments with apartments, markets, schools, playgrounds, shops, hawker centres and an MRT station were planned to house the burgeoning population in an ambitious modernization programme that started in the 1960s. Today, most are state-run and state-maintained but privately owned—a unique public housing concept that is the envy of many foreign governments. They are easily accessible and well worth a wander—even though architecture is functional rather than beautiful, they are well landscaped and well planned and give an important insight into the life of everyday Singaporeans.

Also in the residential sector, but at the high end, is the rise of what may be termed the "tropical modern bungalow". Even though most people live in apartments, there are quite a few houses in Singapore—both old and new—and, since the early 1980s, a number of contemporary Singapore architects has sought to develop a form of architecture that is appropriate to the region's hot and humid climate. In addition to eco retro-fitting its high rises, they have been working on residential forms that trace their roots back to vernacular Malay houses and the colonial bungalow prototype, but use modern construction methods. These experiments have resulted in a plethora of homes in upscale residential areas—eschewing air-conditioning for natural ventilation, using metal or wooden louvres instead of glass curtain walls, incorporating solar power, water and landscaping as cooling devices, and minimizing the impact on scarce environmental resources are some of the devices used. Many such homes feature clean lines, modernist forms and clever sun shading—and the architects are becoming increasingly well known, winning prizes both at home and internationally.

THE BLACK-AND-WHITE COLONIAL BUNGALOW

An important legacy of the city-state's colonial past, the so-called "black-and-white" (above) is a singular design that does not occur anywhere else in the world. Found in various pockets of parkland, the remaining estates are mainly owned by the government and rented to private house-holders. A combination of the mock Tudor half-timbered facade style, popularized from 1900 to the 1930s, and the vernacular Malay house on stilts, the houses are well designed for the Tropics. The upper mainly wooden section absorbs solar radiation less rapidly than a house built entirely of bricks and mortar, while expansive verandahs and overhanging eaves keep heat, glare and rain out. Rattan chicks or blinds encourage breezes or keep tropical elements at bay. Most of the extant black-and-whites date from the 1930s, and for those interested in architecture, there are various tours of these unique houses on offer.

◀ **OPPOSITE TOP** An evening view of the Supreme Court building from above, with the *padang*, Singapore river and Financial District behind.

◀ **OPPOSITE BOTTOM** A night-time view of the aluminium sunshades on the spiky domed Esplanade.

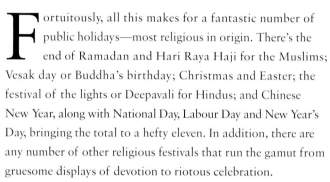

A LESSON IN MULTI-ETHNIC TOLERANCE

Because Singapore is a country of immigrants, it is multi-ethnic and multi-cultural; as such it is multi-religious also. A secular state with a population of Christians, Muslims, Taoists, Buddhists, atheists and agnostics, Singaporeans have a healthy respect for others' views, cultures and religions. Many parts of the world could take a leaf out of Singapore's book when it comes to tolerance. Of course, this does not mean to say that there are not some underlying tensions between the various groups and religions. But, if push came to shove, Singaporeans identify themselves by their nationality first, and their culture, ethnicity and religion after.

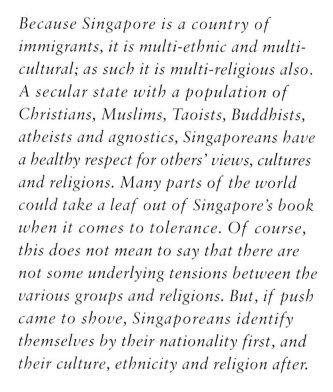

▲ **TOP** Peoples of all cultures and religions are represented in Singapore's devotional centres. Spire and facade of the Gothic-style chapel at CHIJMES (1905). The Masjid Jamae in Chinatown, in rustic architectural style with two symmetrical minarets, built by early Chulia Indians close to 100 years ago. *Gopuram* and entrance to Sri Veeramakaliamman temple (1881), built by Tamil Indians and dedicated to Kali. Below is a selection of Chinese lucky knots and Indian garlands.

▶ **OPPOSITE** A festive golden carriage at the entrance to Sri Mariamman temple, the oldest Hindu temple in Singapore. The six-tiered *gopuram* with elaborate carvings is seen behind.

Fortuitously, all this makes for a fantastic number of public holidays—most religious in origin. There's the end of Ramadan and Hari Raya Haji for the Muslims; Vesak day or Buddha's birthday; Christmas and Easter; the festival of the lights or Deepavali for Hindus; and Chinese New Year, along with National Day, Labour Day and New Year's Day, bringing the total to a hefty eleven. In addition, there are any number of other religious festivals that run the gamut from gruesome displays of devotion to riotous celebration.

Take Thaipusam, for example: Usually celebrated in January or February, this festival is rooted in Hindu legend and was brought to South East Asia by 19th-century immigrants from south India. Entranced devotees, many carrying *kavadis*—intricate steel-and-wood structures attached to their skin by hooks and prongs—form a three-km procession from Little India's Sri Perumal Srinivasa temple to the Chettiar temple on Tank Road. Many of the penitents also have skewers pierced through their cheeks and tongue and are accompanied by a singing, chanting throng that encourages them along the route. Somewhat barbaric to watch, but riveting nonetheless, this is a good example of a celebration where a minority participates, yet is not discouraged by the majority.

Other Hindu festivals include Navarathiri, a nine-day celebration honouring Durga, Lakshmi and Saraswati, the consorts of the Hindu gods, Shiva, Vishnu and Brahma. Visitors are welcome to view the nightly music and dance performances at the various Hindu temples; similarly, they're welcome to watch devotees running across a four-metre-long pit of hot coals at the annual Thimithi festival. Deepavali, the Hindu festival of the lights, is another all-singing, all-dancing affair as Little India celebrates with candles, fairy lights, fairgrounds and fun.

Chinese festivals are obviously dominated by Chinese New Year festivities, where dragon dances and pedestrian parades kick off the new year, but for the most part this is an at-home affair. More vibrant are some of the other Taoist temple festivals, such as the Birthday of Ma Zu, Empress of the Heavens and guardian of seafarers, and the Nine Emperor Gods Festival, held

from the first to the ninth day of the ninth month. The birthday of the Monkey God, held on the 15th or 16th day of the new year, is quite a spectacle: Possessed mediums pierce themselves with skewers and write charms with their own blood, while a sedan chair possessed by the god himself is carried through the streets by worshippers. Close to temples, visitors can watch street opera and puppet shows in makeshift tents.

More cultural than religious is the important Chinese ritual of ancestor worship. The advent of spring is marked by Qing Ming, where homage is paid to the ancestors by cleaning graves and presenting offerings. Equally important is the Hungry Ghosts festival that occurs during the seventh lunar month: during this, operas and concerts are held to entertain the souls of the dead released from Purgatory and vast amounts of fake money, joss sticks and candles are burned outside Chinese homes to appease said souls. Particularly poignant are the often huge effigies of worldly goods such as houses, cars, even full streets that are meticulously made from paper and bamboo—and burnt in one fell swoop.

Many Muslims spend the ninth month of the Islamic calendar fasting in the daytime, so, come sunset, they head to the Arab Quarter to sample the selection of Malay sweetmeats set up on stalls along Kandahar and Bussorah streets at the foot of the Sultan mosque. Particularly celebratory is the end of the fasting month, when street parties and feasts are enjoyed by one and all. The Ramadan bazaar at Geylang Serai is famous for its food, with specialties including *nasi lemak*, *ayam panggang* and Ramly burgers; in addition, there are plenty of stalls selling clothes and souvenirs, so this is a lively option for tourists too.

Even though the island's Christians don't mark their important dates with too much of a song and dance, the run-up to Christmas is marked by a nauseatingly long season of Christmas carols, festive lights and decorations. Orchard Road's main shopping centres vie with each other for the most elaborate Christmas displays and it is a particularly excessive time for shopping.

With so many activities going on in the island's churches, temples and mosques, it is easy to overlook the actual buildings themselves. This would be a shame, as there is much to be viewed in terms of architectural heritage in Singapore's devotional centres. Some of the earliest churches are well worth a visit, while many of the temples, even if they have been re-built or restored over the years, are quite beautiful. The Hindu ones are characterized by tall *gopuram* or entrance towers decorated with a multitude of painted stone statues of deities, while Taoist temples display all the elegance of traditional Chinese architecture: canopy roofs, central courts, *chien nien* friezes, etched calligraphy and fine woodwork. Similarly, some of the Buddhist temples, monasteries and *dharma* centres are wonderful constructions. Take the Buddha Tooth Relic temple built in Tang dynasty architectural style in 2005: It is a popular attraction in Chinatown and serves vegetarian food in the basement.

◄ **OPPOSITE TOP** A devotee lights incense sticks and prays in front of the deity at the Thiam Hock Keng temple. One of the oldest Hokkien temples in Singapore, it was visited by Chinese immigrants giving thanks to Ma Zu (Goddess of the Sea) for their safe voyage.

◄ **OPPOSITE BOTTOM** An Indian family receiving blessings from a Hindu priest during the festival of Deepavali.

▲ **TOP** St Andrew's cathedral (1856–62) was designed by Colonel Ronald MacPherson and serves as the head of the city-state's Anglican mission.

▲ **ABOVE** A dragon dance at the festival of Chingay is a colourful, raucous, noisy affair. This festival involves a procession in honour of the Goddess of Mercy (Guanyin) and forms part of Singapore's Chinese New Year festivities.

EVERY NIGHT IS PARTY NIGHT!

By day, Singapore may be sober and suited, but by night it certainly knows how to let its hair down. With hundreds of pubs, clubs, bars and restaurants, there is truly something for everybody. From plastic tabletop and self-service eateries to slick cocktail joints and pulsating all-night clubs, there's a venue for every taste and wallet.

Naturally, the annual calendar is peppered with events that celebrate having fun. In addition to the various festivals, there are special entertainment programmes that have become annual must-visits in many a visitor's and local's diary. July sees the Singapore Food Festival, where the city-state's multicultural heritage is celebrated in its varied local cuisines; July gets rowers roaring in the Dragon Boat Festival; while the third weekend in September is reserved for the high-octane F1 Grand Prix race and its attendant concerts, parties and productions. Year round, the island of Sentosa and the two integrated resorts stage a variety of shows, music events, all-night dance parties, and more.

For those who visit at other times of the year, it's simply a case of pinpointing your style and budget, and going for it. The only constant is change: what may be here today is also likely to be gone tomorrow. The nightlife scene can be bewildering in that what is hot and trendy one day simply doesn't exist the next. Liberal licensing laws and a wheeler-dealer attitude in the entertainment sector sees a high turnover.

Having said that, there are certain areas offering certain types of nightspot. The Singapore river with its three Quays, namely Boat, Clarke and Robertson, is chock-a-block with clubs,

▲ **TOP** Most visitors will taste the famous Singapore Sling at least once during their stay. Invented in the early 1900s by Ngiam Tong Boon, a Hainanese bartender working at the Long Bar in Raffles Hotel, it has become synonymous with the country.

▶ **OPPOSITE** Every night is a lively night at the quays along the Singapore river: here we see Clarke Quay on the left, Riverside Point on the right and the pedestrianized Ord bridge connecting the two.

watering holes and restaurants. Breezy, open-sided venues are found in the old godowns, merchants' houses and civic buildings that line both banks; in them, you'll find everything from boozy dives to cutting-edge celebrity DJ clubs. Nearby are two streets of old shophouses—Mohammad Sultan Road and Club Street —both of which have become synonymous with nightlife. Often sporting small offices and design houses upstairs, the ground floors have been given over to atmospheric bars and restaurants.

Also buzzy, but less urban, is the rejuvenated Dempsey Hill area where old army barracks surrounded by jungle have rapidly transformed into scores of cocktail bars, cafés and laid-back restaurants. Only a couple of miles from downtown, it's a cool, al-fresco area that offers plenty of chill-out venues, some with live music. Also close by is Rochester Park, a leafy enclave of two-storey colonial bungalows built for the British military and their families; many of these old homes have been turned into wining and dining venues with a heritage atmosphere. More al-fresco is to be had at Holland Village, a popular venue for younger Singaporeans and expatriates. Here, many reasonably priced pubs and eateries spill out into the main street that is pedestrianized at night. There's also a semi-covered food court, a 24-hour *kopitiam* and a wet market.

No section on nightlife would be complete without at least a mention of Singapore's two casinos and their attendant bars and restaurants. Somewhat controversial in planning and execution, these are housed in two "integrated resorts", Marina Bay Sands and the Resorts World Sentosa, both of which began operation in 2010. Before this time, gambling in Singapore was illegal with the exception of the lottery and certain horse races. Ostensibly opened to boost Singapore's tourism industry, the casinos are small in comparison to the hotels, shopping malls, food and beverage outlets and the like that surround them—but exist they do. If you fancy a flutter, they are open 24 hours a day.

◀ **OPPOSITE: CLOCKWISE FROM TOP LEFT** Situated on the rooftop of Singapore's highest office tower, the lively bar aptly known as Altitude has wonderful views over Marina Bay.

◀ Guests at Sarnies, a bar/café on Telok Ayer Street, enjoy both the fresh food made on the spot and chalked up on the blackboard and the convivial ambience.

◀ Each year Siloso Beach on Sentosa island hosts an all-night music and dance party

called ZoukOut. Organized by one of Singapore's oldest and best clubs, Zouk, it attracts top DJs and artists and crowds in the tens of thousands. It has become an annual must-go for clubbers in the South East Asian region.

◀ More action is to be had in Holland Village during most evenings. Bars and restaurants line Lorong Mambong, the main street.

◀ Revellers let their hair down at the annual ZoukOut party —it's not for the faint hearted!.

THE SINGAPORE FLYER

Singapore always aims to do bigger and better, so naturally the Singapore Flyer is the world's tallest observation or Ferris wheel. Rising some 165 metres above sea level (roughly the height of the island's tallest hill, Bukit Timah), it is located at the confluence of Singapore's two rivers—the Kallang and the Singapore rivers—and affords views over the city centre and beyond.

Even though it is 30 metres taller than the London Eye, it looks remarkably similar to its British counterpart. Each of its 28 air-conditioned capsules holds up to 28 passengers and the ride takes just over half an hour. Views from the capsules, especially when at its zenith, are superb. On a clear day, you can see the Indonesian islands of Batam and Bintan to the south, and as far as Johor in Malaysia to the north. You also get an idea of how many boats routinely dock in Singapore's waters. Closer are the areas of Kampong Glam and Marina Bay, as well as the long East Coast Park, while almost directly below is the pitstop for Singapore's Formula 1 Grand Prix race.

Interestingly, when it opened in March 2008, the flyer rotated in a counter clockwise direction when viewed from Marina Centre. However, the intervention of feng shui masters resulted in the direction changing to clockwise on August 4th.

SPECTACLE, SPORT, RECREATION AND RELAXATION

Singapore is keen to market itself as a sporty nation, with a plethora of different spectator and participant sports options. The former category is dominated by the annual F1 race, the world's first Formula 1 race to take place at night, but there are plenty of other choices: Thirty-two weekends each year see horse racing at the Singapore Turf Club, there are various football and rugby tournaments to watch, and cricket matches are to be found on the city centre's padang most weekends. For the participant, there are multiple choices —from running, hiking and cycling, to water sports, racquet sports, bowling and golf.

Each year in the third weekend of September, the downtown area is closed to traffic, the racetrack with its wire crash barriers and lights goes up, and the Marina Bay area revs up for the annual Formula 1 race. Since the first race in 2008, the F1 and its attendant schedule of entertainment events has grown and expanded exponentially, so now it is firmly embedded in every petrolhead's calendar. Not only is the floodlit adrenaline-fuelled circuit an exciting attraction, there is an extensive agenda of rock concerts, VIP parties, exhibitions and race-themed events alongside. A few detractors bemoan the closure of some of the downtown roads, but most agree it is a well-organized, high profile weekend—one that showcases Singapore's ability to put on world-class events with a minimum of fuss and a maximum of panache.

▲ **TOP** Begun in colonial times, horse racing commenced in 1843 in Singapore and was operated by the newly formed Singapore Sporting Club, later to be renamed the Singapore Turf Club. It continues to this day.

▶ **RIGHT** The Singapore Grand Prix takes place on the Marina Bay Street Circuit. It was the inaugural F1 night race and the first street circuit in Asia in 2008. It will remain on the F1 calendar through at least 2017, as the race organizers have signed a contract extension with Formula One Management.

Other international events include the annual International Rugby Sevens tournament held annually on the *padang* and several prestigious horse races. Horse racing was introduced to Singapore by the British in colonial times and it remained popular with the local Singaporean community after Independence. The S$3 million Singapore Airlines International Cup, held in May, is one to look out for as it is attended by some of the world's top jockeys, trainers and owners.

Singapore boasts a significant range of affordable sports facilities and, climate aside, it is a great place to exercise. As it is pretty flat, cycling, biking and running trails are plentiful and easy, but there is challenging terrain in the Central Catchment Nature Reserve comprising the MacRitchie, Peirce and Upper Seletar reservoir parks. A particular highlight at MacRitchie is the Tree Top Walk, a freestanding suspension bridge that forges through the canopy and offers fantastic views of plants and animals in the forest—if you're lucky you may catch sight of a long-tailed lemur "flying" from one tree trunk to another.

Some of the island's parks offer more than flora and fauna in the form of history: Relics of Singapore's involvement in World War II, such as bunkers, machine gun posts, forts and the like are all retained in Labrador Nature Reserve, Sentosa and Fort Canning. A hilltop fort in the latter served as the Malayan Command post in 1941 and one of the bunkers now houses a small, but hi-tech, museum called The Battle Box: in this maze of 26 underground rooms and tunnels, visitors are transported back to 15 February 1942 when Singapore fell to the Japanese. A combination of animatronics, computer-generated special effects and "real" exhibits such as Japanese codes etched onto the walls brings those last disastrous days of the war to life.

For a land-strapped country, Singapore boasts a huge number of golf courses and several of them are world-class. Many of the clubs open their tees to visitors, but fees are high and weekends are busy. Nonetheless, it is not hard to get a game. And, as is to be expected of an island, water sports abound: Sailing, wind surfing, wakeboarding, kayaking and more are all available both in the sea and in certain reservoirs.

Many people in Asia have benefitted from a regular session of reflexology as part of their weekly routine for decades, but in recent years this phenomenon has branched out with the introduction of the spa, a facility that offers massage, beauty treatments and all manner of therapeutic offerings. Singapore is no exception—in fact, nearly every street seems to have a spa that promises to relax or rejuvenate you, for a fee. A newish craze is the fish spa, where small fish nibble the dead skin from your feet: for some reason, this has proved highly popular in Asia. There is even a fish spa at Changi airport if you want a final spa experience before you head home.

▲ **ABOVE** A floating platform, the size of a football pitch, is used for spectacles in Marina Bay.

◄ **OPPOSITE: CLOCKWISE FROM TOP LEFT** Run by the Singapore Dragon Boat Association, there are a number of annual regattas, for enthusiasts. Here the boats line up at the dock in Marina Bay.

◄ The 250-metre Tree Top Walk provides wonderful views for nature enthusiasts as well as a decent workout as the round trip walk takes about two hours. It also plays an important role in forest canopy research, furthering our understanding of how forest ecosystems work.

◄ The Singapore Turf Club hosts all the island's horse races. Here, a potential winner breaks away from the rest of the competitors.

◄ Although an elite sport, polo has a long history in Singapore, with the first matches played in the centre of the old race course on Bukit Timah. With the advent of the Singapore Polo Club in 1886, the sport became more popular. Today, the Polo Club hosts many tournaments at its leafy Mount Pleasant premises.

◄ As well as acting as a fresh water reservoir, Marina Bay often hosts watersports such as this Aberdeen Extreme Sailing event held in April 2013. The Korean entry is pictured here.

THE HISTORIC CITY CENTRE

From the landing site of Sir Stamford Raffles to the collection of stately civic buildings clustered around the padang or cricket pitch, an exploration of Singapore's colonial core is essentially a trip down memory lane. Numerous monuments, churches, galleries, museums, parks and more all stand testament to the nation's rich and varied history.

Visitors keen to experience Singapore's colonial history and learn more about its various inhabitants should not miss out on a trip to Empress Place situated at the mouth of the Singapore river. An impressive neo-Palladian edifice that used to house government offices, it was built to catch the attention of immigrants and visitors sailing into Singapore harbour. Then it was a potent symbol of the power and affluence of Empire; today it houses the pioneering Asian Civilisations Museum (ACM). Beautifully restored, its austere cream walls and pitched roofs form a graceful backdrop to the river on one side and the Victoria theatre and the *padang* on the other. In addition to the museum, it houses a couple of swanky restaurants and bars fronting the river.

Seeking to promote a better appreciation of Singapore's multi-ethnic society in the context of pan-Asian cultures, the ACM has 10 thematic galleries filled with over 1,600 prized artifacts to illuminate the story of Asia. In addition, there are plenty of bells and whistles in the form of state-of-the-art technology—interactive hosts, projected videos and images, ambient sound and lighting—giving the museum experience a multi-layered richness.

Adjacent the museum on the riverfront, one may view a statue of Sir Stamford Raffles, placed at the spot where Singapore's founder is believed to have first landed on 29 January 1819. A replica of the original bronze statue by sculptor-cum-poet Thomas Woolner that was housed firstly on the *padang*, then later in front of the Victoria Memorial Hall, it was placed here on the 150th anniversary of Singapore's founding. Adjacent is a stand of travellers' palms: often called the symbol of Singapore due to their ubiquitous presence in seemingly every park and roadside planting, they are in fact native to Madagascar.

Next along up the river, are the new and old government buildings—Old Parliament House, now an arts centre, and the newer present-day parliament. At the northern flank

▲▲ **PREVIOUS PAGE** The glamour of Marina Bay at night is encapsulated in an iconic floodlit view.

▲ **TOP** The War Memorial or "Chopsticks" (1967). The Gothic-style chapel (1901–04) at the CHIJMES complex. The Arts House at the Old Parliament with a statue of a bronze elephant in foreground. This was a gift from King Chulalongkorn of Thailand, as a token of appreciation after his stay on 15 March 1871.

◄ **OPPOSITE** The famous statue of Sir Stamford Raffles in front of the Victoria Theatre.

of the *padang* lie the old Supreme Court, the Norman Foster-designed courthouse (2000–2005), City Hall with a classical façade of Corinthian columns, and the graceful outline of St Andrew's cathedral. It is just adjacent the CHIJMES complex, a pragmatic example of architectural re-use. Previously home to a chapel, convent school and convent quarters with a history spanning 130 years, the site has been restored and reinvented as a shopping, dining and entertainment centre. Comprising a number of colonnaded, cream-coloured buildings set around a central patch of green, it is known for its night market and outdoor jazz concerts.

Newer additions to this area are the war memorial, Suntec City and the Esplanade concert and theatre complex. Known locally as the Chopsticks, the war memorial is composed of four identical pillars, each 70 metres high, thrusting high into the sky. Designed by Leong Swee Lim of Swan & Maclaren architects to pay tribute to the many civilians who were killed during World War II, it was intended to represent the four major ethnic groups in Singapore—Chinese, Malay, Indian and other races. As such, it is highly relevant today in a country that prides itself on its ability to integrate different peoples.

At its southeastern flank you cannot miss the four towers and squat façade of Suntec City, Singapore's most prestigious convention and exhibition venue. At its centre is the so-called Fountain of Wealth, the world's largest fountain and site of a laser show every evening. As it is built on feng shui principles, people flock to the site in the hope that some of the good luck and energy from the waters will rub off on them. Certainly if you fancy a bit of shopping and you are there in the early evening, it's worth a look.

Located a short walk uphill from the civic district is a small hill now known as Fort Canning Park. Once called Bukit Larangan (Forbidden Hill), as the ancient kings of Singapura are said to have ruled the island from here, it houses the tomb of the last king, Sultan Iskandar Shah, the remains of a British fort dating back to 1859, an early European cemetery, and a couple of colonial-style buildings, as well as areas of parkland and a spice garden. A breath of fresh air from the muggy downtown streets, it is now the venue of choice for outdoor evening events—rock concerts, the WOMAD festival, and Ballet under the Stars performances, amongst others.

The park was named after Viscount Charles John Canning, one of Singapore's mid 19th-century Governor Generals and the first Viceroy of India. Under the British Army, its hilltop fort served as a military headquarters, with Lieutenant-General Arthur Ernest Percival establishing his Malayan Command post here in 1941. One of the bunkers now houses a small, but hi-tech, museum called The Battle Box: in this maze of 26 underground rooms and tunnels, visitors are transported back to 15 February 1942 when Singapore fell to the Japanese. A combination of animatronics, computer-generated special effects and "real" exhibits such as Japanese codes etched onto the walls brings those last disastrous days of the war to life.

◀ **OPPOSITE: CLOCKWISE FROM TOP LEFT** A statue of Sir Stamford Raffles bears the inscription "On this historic site, Sir Thomas Stamford Raffles first landed in Singapore on 29th January 1819, and with genius and perception changed the destiny of Singapore from an obscure fishing village to a great seaport and modern metropolis".

◀ An exterior view of the spire of St Andrew's Cathedral. The building was said to have been inspired by Netley Abbey, a ruined 13th-century church in Hampshire, UK.

◀ Along with adjacent City Hall, the old Supreme Court building is currently undergoing transformation into a new National Art Gallery slated to open in 2015.

◀ A view of the *padang* and Cricket Club, with a game of cricket being played.

▲ **TOP** The old Tao Nan School building (1912) on Armenian Street houses the informative Peranakan Museum.

▲ **ABOVE** Brightly coloured shutters on the 1934 MICA building which today houses a number of art galleries.

Completing the colonial core's cultural edifices are the National Museum, the jewel in the crown of the National Heritage Board's collection of museums, the Peranakan Museum and the Singapore Art Museum (SAM). The National Museum is located in a 19th-century neo-classical edifice with a cutting-edge modern extension at the back and is an imposing sight. Inside, a wide variety of multimedia exhibits presents the story of Singapore, a potted historical and cultural tour of the city-state, as well as the so-called eleven National Treasures. In addition, there are visiting exhibitions, a series of performances and film screenings, a dynamic Night Festival, and some visually arresting art installations.

Ten galleries showcasing the cultural, business and social life of the unique Straits Chinese form the basis for the Peranakan Museum, while SAM is housed in a restored 19th-century mission school. Showcasing both historical and contemporary art from within the South East Asian region, the gallery also hosts visiting exhibitions obtained through strategic alliances with international arts and cultural institutions.

USEFUL INFORMATION
MAP REF: E4
City Hall and Esplanade MRT stations.
Public bus: Numerous buses.
http://www.acm.org.sg (K9)
http://www.theartshouse.com.sg (K9)
http://www.chijmes.com.sg (K8)
http://www.sunteccity.com.sg (L8)
http://www.thebattlebox.com (J8)
http://www.nationalmuseum.sg (K8)
http://www.peranakanmuseum.sg (K8)
http://www.singaporeartmuseum.sg (K7)
http://www.raffles.com/singapore (K9)

◄ **OPPOSITE: CLOCKWISE FROM TOP LEFT** The National Museum of Singapore, originally built by Colonel Sir H E McCallum in 1887 as the former Raffles Library and Museum.

◄ An aerial view of the *padang* and Cricket Club, with colonial buildings and river behind.

◄ The clock tower and Victoria Theatre and Concert Hall with national flag flying above.

◄ An interior view of the nave of St Andrew's Cathedral features soaring arches in the neo-Gothic style. It was built by Indian convicts to a design by Colonial Secretary Ronald MacPherson.

◄ The Fort Canning Centre in Fort Canning, previously the barracks of the British Army and currently a venue that can be hired out for a variety of functions.

◄ A cast iron fountain imported from Glasgow around 1890 which used to be a prominent landmark on Orchard Road. After it was found in pieces in the garden of a Singaporean family, it was donated to Raffles Hotel, where it currently sits in a courtyard.

◄ Night view of the façade of the Singapore Art Museum, the former St Joseph's Institution building.

RAFFLES HOTEL

Pretty much every visitor to Singapore will enter the porticoed entrance of Raffles Hotel, either to stay in one of its capacious suites, to sample a Singapore Sling (invented in the Long Bar in 1910) or a curry in the Tiffin Room, or simply to wander through its colonnaded corridors and courtyard gardens. Opened in 1887 as a 10-room bungalow hotel, then rebuilt in 1899, its early 20th-century heyday was punctuated by glittering balls, glamorous dinner dances, and visits by many a distinguished visitor to the Far East. Somerset Maugham called it a symbol for "all the fables of the Exotic East" and, today, a suite with personalized letters from the writer and photos of him in residence is named after him.

This sense of history (and myth) lingers on: A photo of Ava Gardner who stayed in the hotel in the 1950s exudes high-life Hollywood glamour; a pre-dinner drink in the Writer's Bar brings to mind Conrad and Coward, cocktails and colonialism, a heady mix if ever there was one; and evidence of the Sarkies brothers' legendary hospitality is to be found everywhere: Rudyard Kipling was a fan, as was James Michener who remarked "to be young and have a room at Raffles was life at its best".

Designated a National Monument in the late 1980s and meticulously restored before its grand reopening in 1991, the hotel is a fine example of how modern-day Singapore embraces its past, yet looks firmly towards the future. Its combination of quality service and oriental opulence are beguiling indeed.

NARROW LANES, SHOPHOUSES AND TEMPLES

Singapore's Chinatown, sandwiched between the Singapore river and the thrusting high-rise Commercial District, is an atmospheric area of narrow streets lined with shophouses, temples, mosques and markets. It probably looks remarkably similar to when it was originally constructed to specifications drawn up in Raffles' 1822 Ordinances. Today, despite urbanization, the authorities have managed to conserve vast tracts of the area—some more successfully than others.

▲ **TOP** The dragon, popularly used in Chinese New Year celebrations, is a symbol of success and power. Lucky knot. A selection of roast ducks hanging from hooks. *Char siu bao* or Cantonese barbecued pork-filled buns.

▶ **OPPOSITE TOP** The Thian Hock Keng temple, the oldest and most important Hokkien temple in Singapore sports dragons frolicking on the roof. The name translates as the Temple of Heavenly Bliss.

▶ **OPPOSITE BOTTOM** One of the courtyards in the same temple overlooks the shrine of Ma Chu Po'h.

Many people start their Chinatown exploration on Telok Ayer Street, a gently curving road that once ran along the shoreline of the Straits of Singapore. Today, as a result of Singapore's huge land reclamation programme, it is quite far inland—but many of the temples and mosques that immigrants flocked to on arrival to give thanks for safe passage still remain.

Unfortunately, the northeastern end of the street has lost almost all its old-style character as it is fronted by Far East Square, a block of heritage buildings that has been gentrified into a type of pseudo conservation project for tourists. Amidst the cafés, pubs, shops and kiosks, it's worth popping into the Fuk Tak Chi Museum: originally established in 1824 by Hakka and Cantonese communities as a temple, its architecture is intact, but its atmosphere sadly lacking. Amongst the 200 or so exhibits donated by various residents of Chinatown is a unique model depicting the streets and activities along what would have been the 19th-century Telok Ayer shoreline.

Next up is the Nagore Durgha shrine at the junction of Boon Tat and Telok Ayer Streets. Mixing Palladian and Indian Moslem styles with symmetrical precision, it was built in 1830 to commemorate the visit of Shahul Hamid Durgha, a holy man from Nagore. Next door is the magnificent Thian Hock Keng temple or the Temple of Heavenly Bliss: built on the site of a joss house where immigrants gave thanks to Ma Chu Po'h, the goddess of the sea, it was built between 1839 and 1842 and wonderfully restored in 2000. Built according to Chinese temple architectural traditions by skilled craftsmen from China, it features stalking dragons on its roofs, elaborately painted doors, intricate *chien nien* friezes, gold-leaf panels and more. Two stone lions flank the entrance, while temple guardian gods are painted on the front doors

Three hundred metres on, you come to the small but popular Al-Abrar mosque. Painted sky blue, it was built from 1850 to 1855

by the *Chulias*, Tamil Moslems from south India's Coromandel coast. And to complete the street's multi-cultural flavour, the southern end of Telok Ayer is home to the East-meets-West designed Chinese Methodist church (1889). The fact that these buildings have survived and continue to prosper so close together is a fitting testament to Singapore's ability to provide succour to all races and religions.

From here, it is a short walk to one of the later streets to be built in Chinatown, Club Street: This is now one of its most popular —a pretty, meandering hill of restored shop- and terrace-houses that was transformed from a near derelict wasteland destined for demolition in the 1990s into a trendy spot to wine and dine.

Club Street may have been named after the old community clubs and associations that historically lined the street, but as these were built piecemeal over a fairly long period of time, this is unverified. What is known, however, is that it was primarily a Hokkien area, famous for its sandalwood temple carving shops, and its shophouses date from the 1890s to post-war additions. Many have been restored and painted in pastel shades over the past two decades; most house wine bars, shops and galleries, although a couple of old-style coffee shops and eateries remain.

Club Street leads into Ann Siang Hill and Road, famous as a remittance hub for early immigrants who wanted to send money and letters home. Today, it has followed Club Street's example: there are a number of Gallic-style wine bars and eateries, as well as two up-market boutique hotels. Imbibe at either of their rooftop bars; the views of the surrounding area are second to none, the atmosphere more than convivial.

A two-minute walk then brings the visitor to Pagoda Street, linking New Bridge and South Bridge Roads, along with parts of Trengganu and Smith Streets. Currently a pedestrian zone, full of shops selling typical Chinatown trinkets, fabrics, Chinese medicines, souvenirs and all manner of tourist tat, it also houses plenty of local restaurants and cafés. For the more culturally inclined, the Jamae mosque (1827) and Sri Mariamman temple (1844) with a pagoda or *gopuram* built over the main gate, are situated at either end. Part of the Chinatown Conservation District, it is also located a stone's throw from the rather exotic-looking, newly built Buddha Tooth Relic temple and museum, dedicated to the Maitreya Buddha.

The westernmost part of Chinatown is known as the Tanjong Pagar area and comprises Tanjong Pagar, Craig, Neil, Duxton and Keong Saik Roads, the latter notorious in the old days for housing the red light district. In 1987, the area was earmarked for "adaptive reuse" and almost overnight it transformed itself into a hub for creative types looking for design studios, small office spaces and/or restaurants and bars. In recent years these have been joined by another couple of boutique hotels: housed in turn-of-the-century classically-inspired shophouse rows in what has come to be termed the "Chinese Baroque" style, they are a welcome addition to the city-state's hospitality sector.

Street Scene, Singapore

▲ **TOP** An archival image of a Chinatown street scene around 1900. A group of hawkers and coolies masses at the junction of Cross Street and South Bridge Road. This is close to Chulia Street, home to many Indians.

◄ **OPPOSITE: CLOCKWISE FROM TOP LEFT** A view of a pub on Ann Siang, one of the streets adjacent Club Street. The area is very lively by night.

◄ A row of shophouses dating from 1927 has found new life as a trendy hotel. The pristine white façade sports elegant Doric columns in the round. There is also an expansive roof terrace.

◄ Imported from China, a selection of colourful silk dressing gowns on sale at a roadside stall in Chinatown.

◄ The interior of a traditional Chinese Medicine shop selling everything from herbal teas to dried fungi, plants, barks and even certain animal parts.

◄ A pair of rickshaws waits for customers on Pagoda Street in the Chinatown conservation area.

◄ An aerial view of the busy shopping arcade in the Chinatown Conservation District. In the old days, this area was full of opium dens.

USEFUL INFORMATION
MAP REF: E4
MRT stops at Chinatown or Tanjong Pagar stations; a little further away, Raffles Place or Outram Park stations.
Numerous bus links.
http://www.chinatown.sg (J10, J11)
http://www.thianhockkeng.com.sg (K10)
http://www.chinatownheritagecentre.sg (J10)

SINGAPORE'S COMMERCIAL POWERHOUSE

In 1819, Sir Stamford Raffles said Britain's aim with Singapore was "not territory, but trade; a great commercial emporium". To this end, he planned for offices and godowns along Boat Quay and in Commercial Square. Today's Financial District, with its gleaming towers and offices, is the direct result of his vision.

Today, the offices around Commercial Square, now known as Raffles Place, have been replaced by high-rise towers running along the two main thoroughfares of Shenton Way and Robinson Road. Predominantly modern, they house the engine that fires Singapore Inc, a thriving financial centre of international repute that offers a broad range of financial services including banking, insurance, investment banking and treasury services. Naturally, firms offering law, shipping, petrochemical and other services jostle for space here as well. In fact, new skyscrapers are going up all the time, many on the adjacent Marina Bay reclaimed area. Called Downtown @ Marina Bay, this is scheduled for completion in 2020.

There isn't a great deal for the tourist to see here: On exiting the MRT at Raffles Place, visitors will likely head for the shops, restaurants and museums at Marina Bay or the funky developments up river (see overleaf). Nonetheless, as an example of how far Singapore has come it is an eye-opener—and there are a few good places to eat and drink.

The Lau Pa Sat Hawker Centre, housed in a lovely filigreed cast-iron Victorian structure, with delicate columns and an octagonal floorplan, is a case in point. Dating from 1894, the open-air building was designed by Public Works Department engineer, James MacRitchie, and erected by Riley Hargreaves & Co with cast iron work imported from Glasgow. Today it has found new life as a lively local food centre, with every variety of hawker fare available. Lunchtime sees the tables packed with suits from the neighbouring offices, while at night the action often spills out onto the southern part of Boon Tat Street. Impromptu satay stalls and other barbecue outlets jostle for business with multicoloured ice *kacang* dessert sellers out in the open air.

USEFUL INFORMATION

MAP REF: E4

MRT: Raffles Place station.

Public bus: Numerous buses.

http://www.clarkequay.com.sg (J9)

http://www.srt.com.sg (J8)

▲ **TOP** Even though Singapore does not have any car manufacturer to date, it is well known internationally for its prestigious airline. Consistently noted for service and style, Singapore Airlines is a truly world-class airline.

◄ **OPPOSITE** Various views of the Financial District and its skyscrapers show the city's inhabitants besuited and ready for work. The photo on bottom right is a lunchtime scene taken within the cast iron Lau Pa Sat Hawker Centre.

BOAT QUAY, CLARKE QUAY AND ROBERTSON QUAY

Singapore's renovated quays—namely Boat, Clarke and Robertson—have been likened to other buzzing waterfront areas such as Darling Harbour in Sydney and the King's Waterfront in Liverpool. Certainly, Raffles would have been happy to see the action here—even if he thought trade rather than play would be the focus.

USEFUL INFORMATION
MAP REF: E4

MRT: Raffles Place and Clarke Quay stations.
Public bus: Numerous buses.
http://www.clarkequay.com.sg (J9)
http://www.srt.com.sg (J8)

▲ **TOP** An amphibious vehicle utilized by the US military in Vietnam is used for a Singapore tour today. An example of public art along the river: Boy Fishing with Dog by Chern Lian Shan. A ticket for the river cruise.

▶ **OPPOSITE: CLOCKWISE FROM TOP LEFT** An aerial view of the Singapore river and quays, with the Financial District behind.

▶ Boat Quay features outdoor seating areas adjacent the river and godown interiors separated by a cobbled lane.

▶ A morning view of Boat Quay with buildings reflected in the still waters of the river.

▶ Futuristic sun- and rain-shades protect the grid of streets behind Clarke Quay.

▶ Bumboat water taxis arrive at the Clarke Quay stop.

In the 19th century, the Singapore river served as the artery for the young colony's trading and commercial activities. It was where many an immigrant first set foot in Singapore, and where most returned to work in the godowns, offices and warehouses in what is today's Boat Quay. The harbour attracted all kinds of craft that plied the trade routes between India and China —and bumboats carried their wares from ship to shore.

As the economy grew, so did development upstream. By the 1860s there were godowns, rice and saw mills, boatyards, up-scale homes and offices on both sides of the river; and, after the turn of the century, the development continued on and up. Clarke Quay and later Robertson Quay further up on the east side became busy centres of trade with rows of shophouses oiling the wheels of commerce.

It was only after Singapore relocated its port westwards and the pitiful state of the river was revealed that the authorities embarked on a thorough clean-up campaign. The stone walls along the river's banks were repaired, pollution from up-river factories was stopped, and many of the quayside row houses were restored. Fittingly, the bumboats became river taxis, the godowns turned into shops, clubs and restaurants. Once again, the area began to attract people in their hordes—this time tourists and residents intent on having a good time.

One of the best ways to experience the quays is to take a river cruise on a motorized bumboat; or simply hop on and off at the various landing stages. Adrenaline junkies should alight at the southern point of Clarke Quay for a 0 to 200 km in a second ride on the G-Max Reverse Bungy—but be warned, it's not for the faint hearted! If you need something to settle the stomach after, you're in the right place: Clarke Quay is lined with rather ugly plastic mock-water lily riverside seating with a host of bars and restaurants; or head inland beneath futuristic shelters to take in the street bazaars, weekend flea markets and a bit more action. The area is home to quite a few of Singapore's nightclubs—check out local listings for what's on.

Further upstream, Robertson Quay is a bit quieter, a little less frenetic—but again has a number of waterside eateries and bars. It is also home to the Singapore Repertory Theatre, one of Asia's leading English-language theatres, and a number of international hotels.

A NEW CITY CENTRE FOR THE MODERN MEGALOPOLIS

Singapore's newest addition to its expanding downtown landscape is the area known as Marina Bay. Centred around the old harbour, now transformed by the addition of a barrage into the country's 15th reservoir, it lies adjacent the Central Business District and comprises a beguiling combo of water, parkland, walkways and signature buildings, both old and new.

▲ TOP The ArtScience Museum, fronting Marina Bay in the shape of a lotus. The iconic statue known as the merlion. The Singapore flyer.

▶ OPPOSITE A statue of the merlion facing the three towers of the Marina Bay Sands. Spewing water into Marina Bay, it sits at the mouth of the Singapore river.

▶▶ OVERLEAF The helix bridge is pedestrian only; designed by a consortium comprising the Australian architects Cox Group, engineers Arup and the Singapore based Architects 61, it sports four viewing platforms.

Unsurprisingly, the dominant feature is the triple-tower Marina Bay Sands, one of two "integrated resorts" (casino facilities) planned somewhat controversially some years ago by the government to increase Singapore's tourist revenues. Opened in 2010, it was designed by Moshe Safdie and Associates and comprises three elegantly curved 60-storey skyscrapers topped by a ship-like structure known as the Skypark. Housing a huge hotel as well as the longest and highest infinity-edge pool in the country, it is fronted by a low-rise waterfront development with casino, restaurants, and extensive shopping and convention facilities. Also here is the lotus-like ArtScience Museum, designed to showcase the connection between art and science, as well as other modalities such as media, technology, design and architecture.

Turn left or right out of the complex and it is possible to walk a complete circuit round the reservoir. On the immediate right is a curved latticed metal pedestrian bridge, shaped on the design of a double helix; it's meant to resemble the structure of DNA, thereby bringing to mind life, renewal, abundance and growth. Symbolism aside, it's an ingenious and rather attractive structure. From here it's a short hop, past a football-field sized floating platform that hosts such events as the National Day extravaganza, to the double-domed Esplanade complex, the mouth of the Singapore River and group of low-rise restaurants known as One Fullerton.

The former, with its instantly recognizable two bulging domes clad in aluminium sunshades, houses a 1,600-seat concert hall and 2,000-seat theatre. Compared variously to bugs' eyes, hedgehogs, and durians (after Singaporeans' favourite tropical fruit), it seemed to divide the nation into those that loved it and those that hated it. Whatever your opinion of the aesthetics, however, there is no denying that its world-class performing spaces attract a very high quality of international and regional shows.

Things take a heritage turn at this point, with some wonderfully restored edifices that hark back to bygone days. First up is the Fullerton Hotel, housed in the former General Post Office dating from 1928, and the art-deco style Clifford Pier, famous from the 1930s as an important landing point for immigrants and now an intriguing restaurant packed with antiquities. Designed by the Public Works Department, when Frank Dorrington Ward was then the Chief Architect, the pier's roof structure comprises attractive concrete arched trusses in a riband form. Adjacent is the former Customs House, home to the Customs Police from the 1960s onwards, now also a lively F&B centre, and, anchoring all, in unashamedly modern glass-and-steel, is the luxe Fullerton Bay hotel. With spectacular views of the bay and Singapore skyline, the hotel is the work of legendary interior designer Andre Fu. The rooftop bar and swimming pool are well worth a visit.

From here it is round the bay, past some newer gleaming high-rises to the Marina Bay City Gallery, a display of sustainable design features and an interesting little museum in itself. It showcases the technology and planning behind the whole area, as well as future events and developments: perhaps it would be best to start your Marina Bay tour here?

USEFUL INFORMATION
MAP REF: E4
City Hall, Raffles Place and Marina Bay MRT stations or the Promenade and Esplanade Stations on the Circle Line.
http://www.marina-bay.sg (L9)
http://www.marinabaysands.com (M9)
http://www.esplanade.com (L9)
http://thefullertonheritage.com (L9)

◄ **OPPOSITE: CLOCKWISE FROM TOP LEFT** The Singapore Symphony Orchestra plays at the Concert Hall in the Esplanade more than 100 times per year.

◄ The Esplanade Theatres by the Bay complex houses a number of eateries that spill out into the open air at ground level and a library on the third level above.

◄ The annual fireworks display on Singapore National Day lights up Marina Bay in dramatic fashion.

◄ The view across the city from atop the Skypark at Marina Bay Sands is far-reaching. On a clear day, Johor in Malaysia can be seen.

◄ The prow of the "ship" atop Marina Bay Sands hotel comprises a Skypark viewing deck and bar/restaurant.

THE MERLION, SYMBOL OF SINGAPORE

Directly opposite Empress Place on the west bank of the Singapore River is the somewhat incongruous sight of crowds of people milling around a half-lion, half-fish statue spewing water into Marina Bay. Called the merlion (after Singapura meaning Lion City in Sanskrit and the island's connection with the sea), the creature was originally devised as a logo for the Singapore Tourist Board (STB) and somehow has been elevated to become the national symbol of Singapore. In fact, its origins lie in myth: such creatures with the body of a fish and the head of a lion exist in a number of different cultural traditions.

Along with other replica statues dotted round the city-state, including a huge 37-metre edifice on Sentosa island, the merlion attracts tourists wishing to have their photograph taken next to it. This particular statue is the original one and is 8.6 metres tall. Between 13 March to 15 May 2011 during the Singapore Biennale, the sculpture was concealed behind temporary walls and made available as accommodation (above). Guests were charged S$150 per night to sleep in the "room" that included an en-suite bathroom and butler service. This unusual structure was assembled by Japanese artist Tatzu Nishi as an exhibit at the Biennale, which was organised by the Singapore Art Museum.

AN OASIS OF GREEN IN THE CITY

Described by its creator, Dr Tan Wee Kiat, as "a botanic garden masquerading as a theme park", the first section of the Gardens by the Bay is now open. Comprising the 54-hectare Bay South (the other two will be east and north-east of the Marina Bay reservoir), it is a waterfront garden that stretches to the Marina Barrage. Without doubt, Dr Tan has transformed a polluted piece of reclaimed land into a magical garden. The water features, massive horticultural displays, open spaces for performances, two conservatories and a futuristic collection of "Supertrees" are all superlative.

▲ **TOP** The two glass domes at the Gardens by the Bay horticultural extravaganza line the river just above the Marina Barrage.

▶ **OPPOSITE TOP** The interior of the Cloud Forest glass house features a massive "hill" covered in flowering plants. Visitors take a lift to the top, then descend via a walkway.

P art of the National Parks' scheme to establish Singapore as the world's premier tropical garden city, the park is both sustainable and educational. At its heart is a mass of high-tech "Supertrees" (see back endpaper)—spectacular vertical tropical gardens dripping with ferns, orchids, bromeliads and climbers, that double up as solar thermal collectors, rainwater harvesting devices and the like. The tallest even has a bistro at its top, accessible to diners by a lift. They also act as the engine room for two spectacular cooled conservatories—the 1.2-hectare Flower Dome and the 0.8-hectare Cloud Forest.

Central to the Gardens' design concept, the former is an iconic, clam-shaped structure that replicates the cool-dry climate of the Mediterranean and semi-arid subtropical regions. Featuring an uncommon range of flowers and plants such as baobabs, olive trees and date palms, its primary purpose is to tell the story of plants and their intimate relationship with man and the ecosystem. Serving a similar purpose, the Cloud Forest conservatory mimics the cool-moist climate of Tropical Montane regions, with cutting-edge technologies providing the energy-efficient cooling systems, and a 130-foot cascading waterfall amidst an extraordinary collection of wild orchids from Borneo, wild begonias and fuchsias, tropical rhododendrons, and a variety of pitcher plants.

The Horticultural Show Gardens are another highlight: Each of these intricately landscaped gardens is themed to evoke a local style and period and showcase both tropical plants and the history and culture of Singapore's three main ethnic groups, as well as the city-state's colonial heritage. Malay-, Indian- and Chinese-themed gardens, along with displays of lucrative crops and spices, tell the story of Singapore's relationship with its inhabitants and trading partners—and the types of plants, trees and crops they nurtured.

In the first seven months of opening, Bay South has received three million visitors, most of whom seem to leave the area with their jaws on the ground. When Bay East and Bay Central come on board, they will double the area of these unique gardens.

THE MARINA BARRAGE

At the southern section of the park, one finds the Marina Barrage, a dam that is built across the 350-metre Marina Channel to keep out sea water and help boost Singapore's water supply via the creation of its 15th reservoir. Marina Reservoir, together with Punggol and Serangoon Reservoirs, increased Singapore's water catchment area from half to two-thirds of Singapore's land area in 2011. It also serves the purpose of alleviating flooding in the low-lying city areas. The Visitors' Centre adjacent the dam is worth a look—it contains a mine of information and also conducts tours for those interested in the workings of the dam.

A TASTE OF THE SUBCONTINENT

If Chinatown seems a little manufactured, Little India is the absolute opposite. Centred around Serangoon Road, with a maze of shophouse rows radiating out from it, it is the centre for the large Indian community in Singapore. You could be forgiven for thinking yourself in the subcontinent here: from the scent of jasmine garlands and curry powder to the clanging of temple bells and the hordes of young Indian men promenading its streets on the weekends, the area is chaotic, lively and ... well ... Indian in nature!

Start your tour at the Tekka wet market where herb, vegetable and other vendors mingle with stalls selling Malay, Chinese and Indian food—a busy draw at breakfast. *Tekka* translates as "bamboo shoot" in Teochew, as the area was once home to large groves of bamboo. Then, it is just a case of wandering along the crowded five-foot ways and seeing what you stumble across—there's no better way to soak in the atmosphere than to browse at will. Shops selling saris and silks, myriad spices, brassware and other Indian paraphernalia spill out of shops into the covered walkways; all the while you're serenaded by the blast of Indian *bhangra* and Bollywood music.

All ideas of sterile Singapore are banished in this bustling area: there's a fresh yoghurt stall and a man throwing dough into the air to make *roti prata*. People deftly weave flower garlands on the roadside, while souvenir stalls with incense sticks, Ayurvedic oils and *paan* (made from betel leaf, areca nut, gambier and lime) are found at every corner. Bargain hunters flock to the 24-hour Mustafa Centre, the king of Singapore's white goods' stores, while a browse at the Sungei Road Thieves Market, an impromptu collection of jumble stalls, is an eye-opener. In addition, there is an Indian food court and plenty of local eateries—curries served on banana leaves washed down with fresh juices are the order of the day here.

The area is also home to the Sri Veeramakaliamman temple (see opposite) and the Sri Srinivasa Perumal temple, the starting point for devotees during the annual Thaipusam festival (see overleaf). There's also the small Abdul Gafoor mosque in the Moslem colours of green and gold and the late 19th-century Confucian Leong San temple dedicated to Kuan Yin, Buddhist goddess of mercy. In addition, try not to miss the Kampong Kapor Methodist Church with Dutch-style gabled roofs; it was built in 1930 to cater to a mainly Peranakan congregation. As such, the area reflects Singapore's multi-religious population—all are within a stone's throw of each other.

▲ **TOP** A Singaporean Indian woman in a sari. A brightly painted shophouse in Little India sports Malay-style tracery under the roofline. A green parakeet, trained by a Tamil astrologist to pick up Tarot-like fortune cards in order to tell a client's future.

◀ **OPPOSITE** Entrance to the Sri Veeramakaliamman temple, built in South Indian style by Tamil devotees. Dedicated to Kali, the fierce embodiment of Shakti and the god Shiva's wife, Parvati, the temple features an intricately carved *gopuram* with numerous deities.

Architecture buffs should make sure to take in Sam Leong, Petain and Syed Alwi Roads near Jalan Besar: they have some marvellous examples of both Chinese Baroque and Rococo style shophouses with richly ornamented façades sporting all manner of designs: *oeil-de-beouf* (ox-eye) window openings, leafy festoons and garlands, and a profusion of auspicious animal motifs—dragons, phoenixes, prosperity bats, propitious peacocks, protective tigers, long-living cranes and mischievous monkeys.

The ornate Sri Veeramakaliamman temple, found about half way down Serangoon Road, is probably the area's best known landmark. Dedicated to the goddess Kali, its most distinctive feature is its colourful *gopuram* or entrance tower with statues of numerous deities. Kali is the bloodthirsty consort of Lord Shiva (the name "Veeramakaliamman" means Courageous Mother Kali) and she is thought of as a protector. In such a context, it's unsurprising that some enterprising Tamil labourers who worked in the lime kilns that lined Kampong Kapor built a small shrine here as early as 1855. Early carvings and inscriptions gave way to waves of expansion over the decades, with a wooden structure being replaced by the present building with major additions made in 1953 and 1987.

Today's temple is quite large and invariably full of devotees. Visitors are requested to dress appropriately and remove their shoes before entering. Inside there are numerous statues of Kali, with the main statue of the goddess holding a club an addition from South India in 1908. There are also statues of Kali's two sons—Lord Murugan and Lord Ganesha—and a panoply of smaller statues lining the main shrine's ceiling. In addition to its religious functions, the temple acts as a centre for Tamil socio-cultural activities; during the Hindu festival of the lights (Deepavali/Diwali), you may catch a performance of dance and/or music within its walls.

USEFUL INFORMATION
MAP REF: E4
Little India MRT station on Racecourse Road.
Public bus: Numerous buses.
http://www.mustafa.com.sg (L6)
http://www.sriveeramakaliamman.com (K6)
http://www.kkmc.org.sg (L6)

A WALK OF FAITH

The highly symbolic Tamil festival of Thaipusam sees an annual procession of Hindu devotees going between Sri Srinivasa Perumal Temple in Little India and Sri Thendayuthapani Temple on Tank Road. Celebrated in honour of Lord Subrahmanya (also known as Lord Murugan), who represents virtue, youth and power, it involves devotees carrying *kavadis* (heavy spiked offerings) as penance. Many also pierce their tongues and cheeks with skewers and carry a wooden arch across their shoulders. The festival is not just an exclusively Indian affair; several Chinese devotees and people of other races also come to fulfill their vows in this way.

◄ **OPPOSITE TOP LEFT** A shop in Little India, selling colourful *shalwar kameez*, a type of Indian trouser suit.

◄ **OPPOSITE TOP RIGHT** During Deepavali, huge tents selling celebratory gear spring up in Little India. Shoppers browse for decorations and gifts.

◄ **OPPOSITE MIDDLE** A row of shophouses is home to restaurants, jewellers, Indian fashion houses—and more.

◄ **OPPOSITE BOTTOM RIGHT** Attractive lights in the form of peacocks, flames and flowers adorn Serangoon Road during the Indian Festival of the Lights.

◄ **OPPOSITE BOTTOM LEFT** Tourists will find plenty to keep them amused in Little India: Below, an astrologer lays out his cards for a customer; above, a South Indian vegetarian *thali* is served on a banana leaf.

QUIRKY BOUTIQUES AND CAFÉS IN THE ARAB QUARTER

*The golden onion domes of Sultan
Mosque or Masjid Sultan dominate the
area known as Kampong Glam or the
Arab quarter, the centre of Muslim life
in Singapore. Translating as "Village of
the Gelam Tree" in Malay, Kampong
Glam was allocated to Sultan Hussein,
the Malay ruler of Singapore, by Raffles
when he ceded the island to the British.
Even though there don't appear to be
any Melaleuca leucadendron or gelam trees
left in the area, it has been gazetted as
a conservation quarter and retains its
atmosphere of old.*

The area was not only home to the Sultan and his family, but included Arab traders and Bugis, Javanese and Boyanese, as well as Chinese Muslims. As such, it became a thriving commercial centre. Relatively compact, it houses a grid of narrow streets fronted by shophouses and has a charm all of its own. Even though a certain amount of gentrification has taken place, its Arab flavour continues in the myriad of fabric and carpet stores, their colourful wares spilling out onto the five-foot ways. For checked *longyis* and Javanese batiks, there's no better place. There are also plenty of craft and curio shops selling jewellery, baskets, rattan and leather wares, as well as traditional Muslim coffee shops with *sheesha* pipe smoking patrons. Today, however, their neighbours tend to be trendy, independent fashion boutiques and small, funky restaurants. In only a couple of years, the shops on Haji Lane, for example, have transformed themselves into the types of places you'll find in Paris' Le Marais or London's Primrose Hill.

▲ **ABOVE** The pedestrian only Bussorah Walk, flanked by royal palms and colourful shophouses, leads up to the resplendent onion-domed Sultan Mosque.

MASJID SULTAN

Built from 1924 to 1928, Sultan Mosque is oriented in the direction of Mecca instead of aligned with the urban planning grid. Designed by Denis Santry of Swan & MacLaren, the magnificent Indo-Saracenic structure also has Turkish, Persian and Moorish influences. Two gold onion domes, each topped by pinnacles with crescent moons and stars, sit above the east and west façades; the bases of both are ornamented with glass bottle ends that the Sultan collected as donations from poor Muslims. On each corner of the mosque are minarets with staircases.

The east façade hosts the main entrance, accessed via steps leading past tall palm trees on Bussorah Walk. It opens into a lobby where an odd-looking collection of digital clocks displays prayer times; beyond is the two-storey rectangular prayer hall defined by 12 octagonal columns, closed to non-Muslims. A large chamber with mosaic-tiled walls, it houses up to 5,000 people. The west façade entrance facing North Bridge Road is also where you access the mausoleum of Tunku Alam, Sultan Hussein's grandson who died in 1891.

As a national monument and fully functioning place of prayer, visitors are requested to dress appropriately and remove shoes before entering.

Not to be missed is the sultan's *istana* or palace, built in the 1840s to replace Sultan Hussein's original wooden structure. Combining traditional Malay motifs with the Palladian style, it remained in family hands until 2004 when it was acquired by the government and fully restored as the Malay Heritage Centre. Eight galleries showcase Malay history and culture and there is a reconstructed Malay *kampong* house upstairs. The adjacent 1920s Rumah Bendahara (House for the Chief Minister), originally the home of Tengku Mahmud, the heir apparent to the Sultan's throne, was also restored. A neo-Palladian edifice, with an entrance guarded by two eagles, it was re-named Gedung Kuning (Yellow Mansion) and turned into a restaurant.

Overall, Kampong Glam's vibe is quite funky, the atmosphere a unique amalgamation of the old and the new. Even though Singapore's Arabs, descended from Yemeni traders, have long been integrated into the city-state's multi-ethnic population through inter-marriage, a little piece of their history lives on in this attractive area. A particularly good time to visit is during the Ramadan month, when Kandahar Street comes to life after mid afternoon with a collection of bustling food stalls selling tempting *halal* delicacies.

USEFUL INFORMATION
MAP REF: E4
Bugis MRT station.
http://www.malayheritage.org.sg (M7)
http://www.sultanmosque.org.sg (M7)

▶ **OPPOSITE: CLOCKWISE FROM TOP LEFT** Some of the quirky items on display at a Kampong Glam shop.

▶ Gold jewellery and other decorative items on sale for the Muslim community in Bussorah Walk.

▶ A selection of cloth from Basharahil Bros, a dealer in textiles and batiks, which has been on Arab Street for over 50 years. One of the old, retro-style stores in Kampong Glam, it is well worth a visit.

▶ A magenta and turquoise hued restaurant on Haji Lane is representative of the type of trendy F&B outlets found in the area.

▶ A young couple stroll along pretty Haji Lane, looking for bargains. A few years ago, Haji Lane was a narrow strip of near derelict shophouses. Now those same buildings have been renovated and turned into small retail outlets stocked with offbeat, indie labels not found in the usual Singapore malls.

▶ A Haji Lane shopfront sports an individual air with a façade adorned with colourful artworks and unusual sculptures.

▶ Dining in the five foot way of a casual eatery painted in wonderfully eclectic colours.

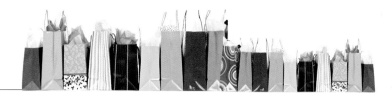

SINGAPORE'S HIGH STREET, PAST AND PRESENT

Orchard Road is to Singapore what Oxford Street is to London and Fifth Avenue to New York—one long line of malls and hotels with shopping arcades that seem to go on endlessly. Constantly packed with pedestrians zigzagging from mall to mall, it is simply called Orchard by locals. But be aware that it is invariably crowded, especially during weekends and evenings, so mornings are best. Once you come up for air, there is no shortage of restaurants, bars, cafés and food courts in which to re-fuel.

USEFUL INFORMATION
MAP REF: E4
Orchard, Somerset and Dhoby
Ghaut MRT stations.
http://www.orchardroad.org (E4)
http://www.istana.gov.sg (J6)

▲ **TOP** Even though it seems unlikely, some shopaholics have been known to carry this number of bags!

▶ **OPPOSITE: CLOCKWISE FROM TOP LEFT** The imposing entrance to Ngee Ann City (1993), a building that has two office towers and five floors of retail.

▶ Chinese New Year shopping takes on a new dimension at Orchard with whole floors in malls transformed into food and gift stalls.

▶ The entrance to Ion, the newest of Orchard's malls.

▶ Pedestrians pack the pavement outside Ngee Ann City.

▶ A Christmas decoration of a star-strewn horse on the pavement outside Gucci.

▶ A colourful sculpture, "Urban People" by Kurt Laurenz Metzler, outside Ion.

▶▶ **OVERLEAF** Singapore's most famous street lit up by night: On the left is Orchard Central, the tallest vertical mall in the country, and on the right is Orchard Point.

In actual fact, Orchard Road is a 1.5-km one-way stretch that starts at the intersection with Orange Grove Road, then runs south east past three MRT stations (Orchard, Somerset and Dhoby Ghaut) to end at the intersection with Handy Road where it becomes Bras Basah Road.

It was not always thus, originally being the site of nutmeg and gambier plantations as well as fruit orchards—hence the name. By the early 20th century, it had become a prime residential area in Singapore: A rare 1880s view shows it as a tranquil country lane, but by the 1920s that idyllic scene had been replaced by rows of shophouses. Post war, most of these were gradually replaced by modern blocks and, by the 1980s, it had become the most sophisticated street in Singapore. The development continues to this day: in 2009, a S$40 million government facelift replaced street lamps, paving and planter boxes, and both 2010 and 2011 saw the openings of new or revamped malls.

If shopping is your thing, this is the place to head. Every single designer label is represented, often multiple times, and you can literally shop until you drop. ION, at the junction of Tanglin and Scotts, is one of the latest high-profile malls to rear its swanky head. Clad within a futuristic curvilinear glass-and-metal façade, it houses 400 shops over eight floors (and that's not mentioning its 60-floor tower of prestige apartments behind). 313@Somerset is another recent addition: its fashion-forward vibe is proving popular with the teen and 20s market. Older favourites, such as Tangs Department Store (founded in 1932 by entrepreneur C K Tang) haven't stood still either: Often called Singapore's Bloomingdales, it brokers tastes between East and West in considerable style these days.

Yet Orchard isn't all about shopping. Approximately half way along its length is the entrance to Emerald Hill, where a number of bars and restaurants are housed in an enclave of shophouses. It's definitely worth a detour and a stroll around, as further up the hill you'll find some fine examples of the elegant Chinese Baroque architectural style. Similarly, take some time to pause by the entrance to the presidential palace or Istana, whose leafy grounds are open to the public a couple of times a year. Opposite is a small park with an impressive water feature.

A WORLD-CLASS COLLECTION OF TROPICAL PLANTS AND FLOWERS

The Botanic Gardens, a 57-hectare splash of green at the northern end of Orchard Road, is full of surprises. Seemingly every year it takes on an expanded form—reinventing itself with new and exotic plantings, water bodies and recreational spaces. As such, it is a vibrant part of the city-state's quest for innovation. It has even requested UNESCO Heritage status.

▲ **TOP** A haven of flora and fauna, the Botanic Gardens attracts both birds and bird photographers. Orchid aficionados will be delighted by the variety of species and hybrids.

▶ **OPPOSITE: CLOCKWISE FROM TOP LEFT** A wooden bridge negotiates a path over a waterway adjacent the main lake.

▶ One of the older structures in the gardens, this gazebo—known as the Bandstand—has had music played from it since the 1930s.

▶ A path in the National Orchid Garden is protected by man-made arches festooned with epiphytic hanging tillandsias.

▶ A restaurant adjacent the one-hectare Ginger Garden is aptly named Halia, the Malay word for ginger.

▶ Two man-made waterfalls: The first is a weir-like structure near the main entrance, the second, made from artificial rocks, is opposite Halia.

▶ Crowds gather to picnic and listen to a concert on the Shaw Foundation Symphony Stage on Symphony Lake.

Founded by an agri-horticultural society in 1859 on a 24-hectare site, the gardens were later handed over to the government for maintenance. During the early days, their function was purely recreational, but by the 1870s they became a centre for scientific research as well. It was here that "mad Ridley", one of the garden's directors, devised propagating and tapping methods on imported Brazilian rubber tree seedlings; he then went on to persuade reluctant coffee growers to switch plantation crops—and changed the face of South East Asia for ever. Later directors started the acclaimed Herbarium, pioneered orchid hybridization and introduced other commercial plants including the ubiquitous oil palm.

The original landscape of a scenic lake, a Victorian-style bandstand on top of a terraced hill, and beds of brightly coloured ornamentals connected by a series of pathways still exists today. Now, however, there is also a micro rainforest area, a section devoted to the growth and display of *penjing* (bonsai) specimens, a valley of exotic palms with lake-fringed stage, an "evolution" garden displaying some of the planet's earliest plants, a marsh garden of papyrus, a ginger garden filled with 300 related specimens of a family that includes lilies, turmeric, and even bananas … and more. Much more. Everywhere you go, you'll stumble across some horticultural wonder or another.

Early morning joggers and groups of Singaporeans practice martial arts and couples picnic in the grounds. Musical concerts are held, and sculptures by international artists are dotted throughout. The National Orchid Garden, covering three hectares of naturally landscaped hillside, houses regular displays of more than 700 dazzling orchid species and 2,100 hybrids, many bred in the garden themselves. The VIP section contains hybrids named after various dignitaries. And for those below 12 years of age, there's the Jacob Ballas Children's Garden: a relatively recent addition, it cultivates an appreciation for nature through interactive exhibits, play and exploration. Outdoor puzzles, a maze and a potting garden that pumps water everywhere are fun attractions. Be sure to bring towels and swimming costumes or a change of clothes for the littlies.

Volunteers run free guided tours of different areas of the gardens every Saturday and there is a Visitor Centre near Nassim Gate. However, many people simply opt to wander down random paths and see where they end up. The gardens' mission is to "connect people and plants"; you'll find that's exactly what happens.

A stone's throw away from the Botanic Gardens is the "lifestyle zone" of Dempsey Hill. Set within a leafy enclave that once housed British military barracks, it is now all buzz and bustle: within a tropical jungle environment, the low-rise blocks have been transformed into bars, restaurants and high-end delis, along with home furnishing stores, spas and other retail destinations. Some may just about make out the Central Manpower Base of Singapore where young men came to report for National Service and the old parade ground, but to most this is a lifestyle and nightlife destination. Galleries and bars, eateries and homeware stores jostle for clientele in low-level converted blocks. And, since many have al-fresco decks with jungle vistas and a laid-back vibe, it's well worth the taxi or bus ride from down town. Typically, there's a young crowd with an appreciation for live music, laughter and good food.

USEFUL INFORMATION
MAP REF: D3
Botanic Gardens MRT station for entrance to North Gate.
SMRT bus numbers 75, 77 and 106 for main entrance.
Free shuttle bus service to Dempsey from bus stop
by Gleneagles hospital, in front of Thai Embassy,
from Four Seasons Park on Orchard Boulevard and
by bus stop B01.
http://www.sbg.org.sg (D3)
http://www.dempseyhill.com (D4)

◄ **LEFT** Palm Valley, home to
the gardens' palm collection,
contains more than 220 species
planted in a herringbone
pattern. Symphony Lake can
be seen in the distance.

SINGAPORE'S NEWEST TOURIST THEME PARK

Recent years have seen the total makeover of Singapore's southern outpost just south of the city centre. What used to be a somewhat rundown island with second-rate tourist attractions has transformed into a busy beach destination, with plenty of man-made and natural attractions set amongst some genuine rain forest. Adventure rides, underwater parks, museums, a golf course, as well as a plethora of hotels, bars and restaurants, are only some of the island's attractions. As the Tourist Board is keen to tell us with its "Asia's Favourite Playground" strapline, Sentosa rocks.

▲ **TOP** A recreation of the film studio logo sits at the centre of the Universal Studios site. Singapore's tallest observatory tower soars high above Sentosa. Graphic and colourful Siloso Beach sign.

▶ **OPPOSITE** A suspension bridge arches across the sea from the southernmost point of continental Asia to Palawan Beach. The modern blocks behind are part of the up-market Capella hotel.

▶▶ **OVERLEAF** A view over the grounds and pool of the Rasa Sentosa resort to the Java Sea beyond.

Even though the word Sentosa translates as "peace and tranquility", these days the island is anything but. Sure, a holiday atmosphere prevails on its southern beaches, but this atmosphere is more beach crazy than beach lazy. Imported sand, breakwaters of stone and greenery, and scores of introduced palm trees give Siloso, Palawan and Tanjong beaches the illusion of tropicality, but there's no disguising the fact that this is more shipping lane than swimming lane. Lines of tankers anchored offshore only look beguiling when it gets dark and their lights twinkle on the horizon.

Nevertheless, there is plenty to keep one occupied here. Fake surfing at the Wave House, suspenseful thrills on the MegaZip, a flying fox with a difference, a woosh in a little cart down the Luge for younger clientele … you can even hover suspended in a simulated freefall parachute jump at the ParaJump. If it ticks your boxes, try stepping off a platform into thin air and freefalling gently down to the ground 15 metres below.

For a slightly more educational experience, hire a segway or bicycle or jump on the tram and head up to Siloso Point to Underwater World and Dolphin Lagoon. At the former, an 83-metre moving walkway takes you through colourful reef and ocean colonies where you're invited to immerse yourself in marine life: feeding manta rays and sharks is a highlight. Then take in a performance of pink dolphins and fur seals in an adjacent lagoon—a special extra may be a "Swim with the Dolphins" experience.

Those with an historical bent may enjoy a detour to Fort Siloso, Singapore's only preserved coastal fort. Home to the nation's largest collection of World War II memorabilia—original guns, canons, old tunnels—it also features interactive exhibits that recreate the drama of the past. Combine this with a look at the Images of Singapore museum and you'll be an instant expert on Singapore's history: Multimedia displays and multi-screen theatre presentations, along with life-sized tableaus depicting local history, illustrate the founding of this multi-cultural nation in all its diversity.

The latest attraction to the island is Resorts World Sentosa, a sprawling casino, hotel and entertainment complex that rises from the northern shore with a brashness that would better befit an urban conurbation than a tropical island. In addition to numerous places to stay and eat, there are a few places to play: First up is the casino, somewhat down market in the basement. You're better off heading to Marine Life Park which in true Singapore style boasts the world's largest oceanarium with 800 species of marine animals and a well-designed waterpark that combines snorkelling and wading with rays with action-packed waterslides. There's also the Maritime Experiential Museum, an educational facility that utilizes technology and interactive exhibits to explore Asia's rich maritime history. You can even take in a 360° theatre experience aboard a sailing ship in a perilous storm ... a journey not for the queasy.

Most popular, however, is Universal Studios, a must-visit attraction for adrenalin junkies. A theme park with some pretty hairy rides, it packs maximum fun into a minimal sized area. Comprising a series of roller coasters based around Hollywood blockbuster themes, as well as a number of movie magic attractions, it is loud, busy, colourful, and relentlessly cheerful. Aimed at the teen market, there are nonetheless some more sedate rides and shows for younger audiences, and plenty of cartoon characters bringing the silver screen to life. And, as is expected these days, there are more than a few interactive experiences to be had.

A recreation of Hollywood Boulevard, framed by palm trees and the stars' Walk of Fame, leads visitors into a series of areas focused on some of Universal's more instantly recognizable movies: *Jurassic Park*, *Return of the Mummy*, *Battlestar Galactica*, *Shrek* and *Madagascar*. Whether you're ducking an army of warrior mummies in total darkness or hanging onto a white water raft on a waterway hurtling through a Jurassic landscape where prehistoric creatures roam free, is immaterial. The knots in your stomach will surely clench the most on the twin-track roller coaster, Battlestar Galactica, that arches above the whole shebang like a pair of oversized twisted spaghetti strands.

Choose between a seated coaster or one where you're suspended upside down, then experience the thrill of the two in tandem, each brushing past the other in a series of aerial near misses. Gravity defying loops and sudden angled turns are only part of the story.

With 24 rides and attractions in total, as well as a plethora of restaurants, cafés and movie-themed shows, such as the Waterworld one based on the futuristic Kevin Costner movie, Universal Studios is easily a full-day experience. It's worth getting there early, as the queues get longer as the day progresses.

▲ **ABOVE AND TOP** Dusk until dawn: The annual ZoukOut party features DJs for Electro, Trance, House, Techno, Mambo, Hip Hop, Pop—and more—on Siloso Beach.

◄ **OPPOSITE: CLOCKWISE FROM TOP LEFT** The Wave House is a recreation of the Californian lifestyle in the Tropics: two "flow waves" for boarding or riding, as well as restaurants, bars and other entertainment.

◄ Younger visitors enjoy the Canopy Flyer ride as they soar over the Jurassic Park terrain at Universal Studios.

◄ Designed by world-renowned golf course designer Ronald Fream, the Serapong Course (1982) is a challenging par-72 championship course.

◄ A four-seater chairlift at the Skyride Luge transports people up a hill so they may descend along a 1.2-km track back to the bottom.

◄ A gigantic recreation of the Far Far Away Castle from the movie *Shrek* is one of the attractions for younger visitors at Universal Studios.

◄ The mostly underground Underwater World at Sentosa opened in 1991 and has more than 2,500 marine animals comprising 250 species from different regions of the world. Highlights include diving in its waters and feeding the rays.

USEFUL INFORMATION
MAP REF: D4
HarbourFront MRT station, followed by Sentosa Express bus from Lobby L of VivoCity shopping mall, or RWS 8 bus outside VivoCity shopping mall. An alternative, offering scenic views over Keppel Harbour and the island, is to take the cablecar from Mount Faber Park.
http://www.sentosa.com.sg (F4–H5)
http://www.rwsentosa.com (F4)
http://www.mountfaber.com.sg (D4)

A FUNKY CITY DISTRICT OFF THE BEATEN TOURIST TRACK

In the last couple of years the Tiong Bahru area has gained kudos as a bit of a hip neighbourhood—less "ang mo" than Holland Village, not so overpriced as gentrified Chinatown, and, unlike the heartlands, without a tower block in sight. As a result, graying uncles and aunties have been joined by a cooler, younger crowd and the odd tourist or two.

USEFUL INFORMATION
MAP REF: E4
MRT: Tiong Bahru.

▲ **TOP** Tiong Bahru was renowned as a neighbourhood of bird-singing aviaries, with bird lovers congregating together over tea and coffee amidst the melodious chirps of their robins, prinias and shrikes. Even though the area known as Bird Corner has been torn down, you'll still see men with their bird cages in the area.

▶ **OPPOSITE: CLOCKWISE FROM TOP LEFT** The funky Forty Hands café, a popular haunt for coffee, is refreshingly loft-like inside.

▶ Low-rise apartment blocks are separated by lawns in the front and narrow lanes behind.

▶ Rounded staircase in art-deco style in one of the low-rise apartment blocks.

▶ The hawker centre is known island-wide for its different stalls. This Chinese-inspired *lor mee* dish costs a couple of dollars.

▶ A typically busy lunchtime scene in the circular hawker centre which has a wet market below.

▶ The triangular market building is clearly visible at the centre of Tiong Bahru. For many years the area was referred to as Mei Ren Wu (translating as "den of beauties"), as many rich men housed their mistresses here.

In fact, these days, you're as likely to hear the sounds of Western indie music as the traditional clash of Beijing opera and the sounds of singing birds. As such, the area has a quirky charm all its own: The streets are named after Chinese pioneers of the 19th and early 20th centuries (Lim Liak, Kim Pong, Guan Chuan, Chay Yan, etc) and the low-rise architecture is a mix between Streamlined moderne and the local Straits Settlements shophouse. Built before World War II by the Singapore Improvement Trust (SIT), they pre-dated the HDB and feature rounded balconies, flat rooftops, spiral staircases and lightwells. Thankfully, 20 blocks were gazetted for conservation in 2003 and there's even talk of the area becoming a UNESCO National Heritage Site—if anything sends housing prices up, that'll do it.

At its centre is Tiong Bahru Market, a 2006 building that is located on the same site as the area's original Seng Poh Market. Circular in form, it houses market stalls on the ground floor and some of Singapore's finest hawker stalls on the upper open-air storey. Well organized with several sections—meat, veg, fruit, flowers, cooked food, even household goods and clothes—it's a colourful spot with a lively crowd on the lookout for a bargain. Accessed by escalators, the myriad of hawker stalls above overlooks a central garden and the wet market below. It attracts foodies from all over the island.

Breakfast with the locals comes highly recommended: Try *chwee kway* (small steamed rice cakes with a garlic turnip topping), *lor mee* (yellow noodles in dark sauce with a touch of rice vinegar) and deep fried fish balls, all washed down with dark thick sweet Indonesian coffee. K F Seetoh's *Makansutra* is a handy reference guide to the best stalls and various delicacies.

Afterwards, take a stroll round the estate. Galleries, a trendy bookstore, Western coffee clubs, upscale restaurants and cute boutiques now sit cheek by jowl with Chinese provision stores and the wet market. The sense of community living remains in the back yards of the Art Deco buildings, while an endearing old-meets-new atmosphere prevails. An area of contrasts, it's well worth a wander.

A DRAMATIC ELEVATED NATURE WALK

Stretching from Singapore's south coast through Mount Faber Park, Telok Blangah Hill Park and Kent Ridge Park, the Southern Ridges is a nine-kilometre trail that is linked by a variety of paths, parks and bridges. Conceived by the Urban Redevelopment Authority (URA) in 2002, it took two years to link the parks at a cost of S$25.5 million.

Useful Information
Map Ref: D4
Harbourfront MRT for Mount Faber Park and Labrador Nature Reserve (plus bus 408 for the latter), Telok Blangah MRT for Telok Blangah Hill Park, and Kent Ridge MRT for Kent Ridge Park.
http://www.mountfaber.com.sg (D4)

▲ **TOP** The cable car that connects Mount Faber with Sentosa island gives passengers a bird's eye view of Singapore's city skyline.

◄ **OPPOSITE: CLOCKWISE FROM TOP LEFT** A truly panoramic view is to be had from Mount Faber stretching over Sentosa island.

◄ A stretch of the elevated walkway leading to Kent Ridge Park.

◄ A mural of the Battle of Pasir Panjang is painted on the facade of the Reflections of Bukit Chandu museum.

◄ A sculpture of three life-sized statues of soldiers honours the Malay Regiment and commemorates the lives lost.

▶▶ **OVERLEAF** Connecting Mount Faber Park with Telok Blangah Hill Park, the 274-metre Henderson Waves bridge rises high above Henderson Road.

The idea behind the trail is to encourage walkers and cyclists, and also showcase this potentially less visited area of Singapore. Mount Faber Park, one of Singapore's older parks, is where most people begin the walk. Even though there is a road that winds its way to the summit (104 metres) from where you can take a cable car to Sentosa, there are also plenty of trails such as the Marang Trail that begins at Harbourfront and ends at the summit. It is a mix of steps and trail, so may not be good for the elderly or those with young children.

Mount Faber Park offers splendid views of the southern parts of Singapore and also connects to Telok Blangah Hill Park via a singular pedestrian bridge known as Henderson Waves (see overleaf). Consisting of a series of undulating curved "ribs" with a *bakau* timber deck, the design is quite distinctive and has become a favourite landmark with locals. Telok Blangah is known for its cascading bougainvillea terraces, a colourful sight at any time of the year, and the colonial-style Alkaff Mansion, a former trading family's home that has been converted into a restaurant. From here there are a couple of options: continue on an elevated walkway through the canopy or opt for a more rugged trail—both lead to the Alexandra area, famous for its horticultural park.

After a stroll through HortPark, where gardening enthusiasts may collect more than one or two tips for tropical planting, there's a short park connector that links you with Kent Ridge Park. One of the last battles for Singapore was fought on this ridge, so the park contains some World War II memorabilia and a small museum that focuses on the battalion of the Malay Regiment in the Pasir Panjang area during the war. The Reflections of Bukit Chandu museum is accessed by a 280-metre boardwalk that winds through the secondary forest canopy at eye level. Here, you'll be able to see many species of tropical tree—*tembusu*, acacia and Dillenia—in a less landscaped environment.

In fact, Kent Ridge Park is one of Singapore's most beautiful natural areas: there are panoramic views from the ridges and the surrounding vegetation has been left *au naturel*. You may even come across a wild boar ... unlikely, but possible!

LABRADOR NATURE RESERVE

Although this nature reserve is not technically part of the Southern Ridges, it lies at its southern tip and affords picturesque views over indigenous coastal vegetation and out to the South China Sea and the southern islands beyond. Criss-crossed by a number of trails, including a rocky sea path, the 10-hectare reserve has a rich variety of specialized flora and fauna, including over 70 bird species and many trees that can withstand salty sea breezes.

In addition to its plentiful bio-diversity, there are some remaining military installations including machine gun posts, old tunnels and a fort that were installed to protect Singapore's southern shore before World War II. It's a peaceful spot with a pleasant promenade area and lookout deck; at present the seashore and jetty are closed to allow marine life to regenerate after extensive building works in the area.

A WORLD-CLASS BIRD PARK, MUSEUMS AND GARDENS

Situated in the west of Singapore, Jurong is the city-state's industrial heartland with hundreds of factories, HDB tower blocks and industrial estates. Conversely, it also contains great swathes of green forest and a number of tourist attractions, many of which are aimed at families.

USEFUL INFORMATION
MAP REF: C3, B3
Science Centre a six minute walk from Jurong East MRT station; Boon Lay MRT followed by bus nos 194 or 251 for Bird Park; Chinese Garden MRT for the Gardens.
http://www.science.edu.sg (C3)
http://www.snowcity.com.sg (C3)
http://www.birdpark.com.sg (B3)

▲ **TOP** The Jurong Bird Park is home to a flock of Carribean flamingoes. The logo features three colourful parrots.

▶ **OPPOSITE: CLOCKWISE FROM TOP LEFT** The Jurong Bird Park: Friendly parrots welcome a visitor. The Lory Loft simulates north Australian rain forest and houses hundreds of lories and lorikeets. A bird show at the Pools Amphitheatre. Flamingo Lake, home to hundreds of pink-hued Greater Flamingos and Lesser Flamingos, is a tranquil part of the park. Jackass penguins in an outdoor enclosure. A tropical jungle canopy walk.

▶ A pair of pagodas in the Chinese Garden are one of the prime attractions. Pagodas were originally built to store the bones of deceased Buddhists.

▶▶ **OVERLEAF** Graceful arched bridges painted red in the tranquil Japanese Gardens.

The cutting-edge Singapore Science Centre could be the first port of call if you are travelling with children: Twelve galleries of interactive displays cover subjects ranging from marine ecology to space, genetics and the human body. Since it opened in 1977, the museum has captivated both adults and children through its extremely innovative ability to both educate and entertain. The adjacent Omni-Theatre shows hourly IMAX movies about the natural world, while next door the sub-zero Snow City offers an opportunity to temporarily leave the Tropics and enter a winter wonderland. A 60-metre-long snow slope can give hours of entertainment to snow-tubing kids; all the kit is included in the entrance fee.

Another popular attraction in Jurong for all the family is the Jurong Bird Park, a 20-hectare park containing more than 8,000 birds from 600 species. A monorail transports visitors to the various attractions including a Waterfall Aviary with custom-crafted 30m-high waterfall and rainforest landscaping; a lake with flamingoes; a recreation of an Antarctic environment with Penguin Parade; the Lory Loft, the world's largest walk-in free flight aviary; and the unique World of Darkness, where night and day have been switched, thereby allowing visitors to view a variety of owls and other nocturnal birds. In addition, as at the zoo which is run by the same company, a number of bird shows punctuate the day—first up is Breakfast with the Birds at 9am, then other presentations showcasing the skills of birds of prey and other species follow.

Another of Jurong's attractions is the 13.5-hectare Chinese and Japanese Gardens in the vicinity of Jurong Lake. Joined by the Bridge of Double Beauty, they are distinctly different in style. As is to be expected, the Chinese has a number of pavilions and pagodas, along with a large collection of *penjing* (Chinese bonsai) specimens and rock sculptures, while the Japanese is simpler, more zen, in character. Both are pleasant for a quiet stroll, especially in the early evening.

ENGAGING WITH NATURE

It's no surprise that the team behind Singapore's famed Zoological Gardens has gone on to design zoos all over the globe, because this zoo is really one of the world's most spectacular. Covering 28 hectares and bounded by the tranquil waters of the Upper Seletar reservoir, it is home to 2,500 specimens from 315 species, 29 percent of which are rare and/or endangered. The zoo's main draw, however, is its "open" concept —where animals are displayed seemingly without barriers and in a natural setting.

The enclosure design is such that species are divided by moats, vegetation and/or cascading water, all the while embracing nature to create a thoroughly natural, jungle-like feel. Unfortunately, some of the big cats are still caged, but most animals inhabit spacious areas that are designed to replicate their natural habitats. Of particular note are the hamadryas baboon enclosure, a rocky desert-like area simulating Ethiopia's Great Rift Valley environment, and the Fragile Forest bio-dome where ring-tailed lemurs, tree kangaroos, sloths and fruit bats freely frolic amongst giant ferns and other leafy trees. Swathes of fluttering butterflies all around heighten the magical feel here.

▶ **OPPOSITE** The flagship species at the zoo is the orang utans, a collection of which are housed in two unique free-ranging areas full of tall trees and thick vegetation. An island and boardwalk complete the habitat.

The zoo's orang utan breeding programme has created a large community of these gentle creatures and in the mornings you can share their breakfast. Throughout the rest of the day feeding times are staggered at suitable intervals and there are plenty of animal shows. In addition, you can immerse yourself in the diversity of tropical flora —exotic ornamentals, commercial crops, fruit trees and the like are planted in various areas with helpful signboards. As such, the zoo is a great learning environment: utilizing both interactive tools and the joy of getting up close and personal with animals and birds, it preaches conservation in a singularly non-preachy way.

Adjacent the zoo is the Night Safari, a 40-hectare jungle park that allows over 1,000 animals from 120 species from South America and Asia to live out their nocturnal routines, albeit watched by humans (sometimes extremely close!). Three walking trails and/or a tram ride take you through eight geographical zones—likely sightings include big cats, elephants, rhinos, giraffes and antelopes amongst others. As at the zoo, the concept is open plan with moats and cattle grids separating the various areas. Don't miss the Leopard Trail with its resident clouded leopards, *binturong* (Asian bearcats) and Malayan civet cats and the specially designed walk-through netted dome where giant flying squirrels glide across the night sky from tree to tree.

Cultural performances, including tribal dances, fire eating displays and blowpipe demonstrations are a regular feature, as is the slightly unconvincing Creatures of the Night show, an animal performance presented three times per night.

USEFUL INFORMATION
MAP REF: C1, D1
Public bus: no 138 runs to the zoo from Ang Mo Kio MRT, no 927 comes from Choa Chu Kang, no 926 from Woodlands and Marsiling MRTs.
Address: 80 Mandai Lake Road
Tel: (65) 6269 3411
http://www.zoo.com.sg (D2)

◀ **OPPOSITE: CLOCKWISE FROM TOP LEFT** One way to view the shoreline at the zoo is to take a boat ride; as you cruise along, you may spot animals such as monitor lizards and white-bellied sea eagles.

◀ The award-winning Great Rift Valley of Ethiopia zone houses a colony of over 90 hamadryas baboons—watching their social activities is highly entertaining.

◀ One of the highlights of the Night Safari is the Fishing Cat Trail that simulates a nighttime trek through the jungles of Singapore. Here, visitors see native species of animals that either used to or are still roaming Singapore's forests today. Other species include giant flying squirrels found at one corner of the Leopard Trail, while free-roaming Malayan tapirs are usually spotted from the tram ride.

◀ Some of the animal shows and feeding sessions allow visitors to get up close and personal with the animals. The giraffes are a case in point: if these gentle creatures tick your boxes, you can purchase food to hand-feed them.

◀ The zoo's two white tigers are one of the star attractions because of their rarity and uncommon beauty. Their spacious habitat is built so as to resemble a dense jungle clearing; they especially like the pool as they are extremely good swimmers.

KIDZWORLD AT THE ZOO

In addition to the obvious animal attractions, there is a host of playtime options for all-day fun for kids. A mini farm allows them to observe and feed rabbits, goats and horses, while pony rides are always popular. Bring bathers for the Wet Play Area and Rainforest Challenge, two fun outdoor playgrounds, the former involving a number of sprayers, climbers and water-flushed slides and tubes. Children are encouraged to be nosy at the *kampong* house, while the Animal Friends Show brings a barrel of laughs with everyday pets performing some amazing tricks.

RAINFOREST RECREATION RICH IN BIO-DIVERSITY

Part of the Central Catchment Nature Reserve, MacRitchie Reservoir Park is probably the most accessible and popular of the country's four reservoir parks, the other three being Lower Peirce, Upper Peirce and Upper Seletar. Together, the four comprise a protected area of rain forest, quality water reserves and pristine native flora and fauna. A network of trails and sensible management allow for recreation in the form of canoeing, rowing, walking, jogging, bird-watching and more.

USEFUL INFORMATION
MAP REF: E3

Nearest MRTs are Marymount and Bradell, but it is still a taxi ride from both. Numerous buses stop at the main entrance car park.
http://www.nparks.gov.sg

▲ **TOP** Outdoor enthusiasts flock to this park both during the week and at weekends, yet it is still possible to feel alone with nature.

▶ **OPPOSITE: CLOCKWISE FROM TOP LEFT** Facilities have been improved at the reservoir for kayakers—good storage for kayaks and a new pontoon are useful additions.

▶ The HSBC TreeTop Walk provides wonderful vistas to observe canopy life.

▶ An area near the carpark is beautifully landscaped, and includes F&B outlets, water dispensers and facilities.

▶ Some parts of the reservoir are incredibly secluded: it's difficult to imagine the big city a couple of miles away.

▶ A flight of steps leading up from the boardwalk on the eastern bank of the reservoir.

The reservoir was the first to be built in Singapore, after a shortage of fresh water had been noted, debated, discussed, but not acted on—even though Straits Chinese philanthropist Tan Kim Seng had donated S$13,000 in 1857 towards its construction. Numerous delays dogged the project which was eventually completed in 1877 at a cost of $100,000. A further $32,000 expansion took place in 1891 under the direction of municipal engineer James MacRitchie, so in 1922 the reservoir was named after him.

Even though much of Singapore's primary rain forest had been cut down to make way for logging and cultivation before the construction of the reservoirs, the parks are now protected—and patches of original vegetation remain. An 11-km trail round the reservoir is a favourite with joggers, bird-watchers and walkers: varied in topography, it includes sections of boardwalk fringing the reservoir, as well as forest trails and a path fringing the Singapore Island Country Club golf course.

Large monitor lizards, both in water and on land, squirrels and long-tailed macaques are easily seen, but the park is also home to some shyer species, namely lesser mousedeer, pangolin and flying lemur. Birdlife is rich and varied, and informative signboards along the boardwalks point out some of the more commonly seen trees and shrubs. If you're keen on a longer hike, trails do link MacRitchie with neighbouring parks; maps can be downloaded from the National Parks' website.

For a birds-eye view of the canopy and some panoramic vistas as far as Upper Peirce Reservoir, keen walkers are advised to walk the 4.5 km nature trail that leads to the HSBC TreeTop Walk, an aerial 250-m-long suspension bridge. Spanning Bukit Peirce and Bukit Kalang, the two highest points in the park, it soars some 25 metres above the ground. As long as there isn't a noisy school group in the area, this is a wonderful spot to commune with nature.

IT'S A REAL JUNGLE OUT THERE!

One of the first reserves to be established in Singapore in 1883, the 164-hectare Bukit Timah Nature Reserve is a haven for the island's remaining tropical flora and fauna. With a decent network of paths, a mountain bike trail, and an informative Visitor Centre, it gives insight into how the island looked before man arrived.

Named after the island's highest hill at a mere 163 metres (Bukit means "hill" and Timah translates as "tin"), the reserve was established after concerns were raised as to the effects of extensive logging. As a result, there are still some pockets of primary rain forest, plenty of lowland tropical vegetation, more than 840 species of flowering plants and over 500 species of animal. Even though the tigers, deer and leopard are long gone, you're likely to see long-tailed macaques, flying lemur and squirrels—along with a vast array of spiders, beetles, birds and bees. Plants include towering trees, many signposted with English and botanical names, palms and rattans, ferns, orchids, gingers and more.

On the reserve's boundary, there are a few popular climbing sites in disused quarries as well as a 6-km challenging mountain bike trail. Within the reserve itself, the easiest walking route is via the paved track leading from the Visitor's Centre to the top of the hill. This can get quite crowded even during weekdays, so it is worth heading off onto one of the side trails. Ranging in length and difficulty, they offer an albeit brief immersion into the luxuriant, damp and dense equatorial landscape—seemingly a million miles away from downtown. Trails are clearly marked on free maps available at the Visitor Centre.

USEFUL INFORMATION

No close MRT stations. Plenty of buses to Upper Bukit Timah Road, then it is a 10-minute walk to Hindhede Road and the Visitor Centre.
www.nparks.gov.sg

▲ **TOP** Palms and gingers are amongst the species found in the nature reserve.

◀ **OPPOSITE TOP** Named after Danish Civil Engineer Jen Hindhede who established a company that operated a granite quarry here, the Hindhede Quarry is now a serene, tranquil lake at the foot of Bukit Timah.

◀ **OPPOSITE BOTTOM** One of the smaller trails that meanders through pristine vegetation in the park.

PUBLIC HOUSING ESTATES—THE "REAL" SINGAPORE

Providing housing for about 85 percent of Singapore's population, the Housing Development Board's high-rises are typically clustered in small suburban towns. Comprising apartments, schools, markets, shops, parks and/or playgrounds, hawker centres and public transport links, they are collectively known as Singapore's heartlands.

A visit to one of these HDB towns can be an enriching experience. Be it Toa Payoh, Bishan, Ang Mo Kio or Tampines, for example, it offers a glimpse into ordinary Singaporean life—away from the up-market shopping malls, public buildings and office towers. Each is a little bit different, but all showcase the "real Singapore" where old and new, the traditional and the technological, the East and the West intermingle in a complex, but largely successful manner.

Since Independence, the state-run HDB has built over a million units—all high-rise. This is because land-scarce Singapore cannot afford to spread; it has to build up. And, in order to promote racial and religious harmony, each housing block has to have an even distribution of ethnic groups. This has successfully shown that difference in culture and religion can be peacefully respected, observed and even participated in by all equally. Tellingly, most units are privately owned, but state maintained.

Many of the older estates have plenty of mature trees providing shade in public areas, but some have become a little dilapidated with age. As a result, the HDB runs an ongoing improvement programme: Lifts and balconies are installed in units that lack these amenities, for example. All the while, new units continue to be built. A good example of a new and improved HDB estate is The Pinnacle@Duxton: consisting of seven interconnected 50-storey towers, there are two long "sky gardens" on the 26th and 50th floors and extraordinary views over the downtown area.

More traditional HDB estates are found further away from the city centre. All are easily accessed by the MRT and many are serviced by special tours of food centres, shops and more.

USEFUL INFORMATION

http://www.myheartlandsingapore.com

▲ **TOP** Void decks on the ground floor of HDB estates are used for all manner of social interaction. Here two senior residents play a game of Chinese chess.

▶ **OPPOSITE AND OVERLEAF** From the 1960s onwards, the Housing Development Board (HDB) is credited with moving people out of squatter areas and slums to these well-organized satellite towns. All estates are well served with public transport—bus and MRT—and have hawker centres, playgrounds and other facilities.

A BIRD-WATCHER'S PARADISE

Situated in the extreme north west of the island, this is Singapore's only protected wetland nature park. As such, it is an important stop-off feeding point for several migratory birds, especially waders. Nonetheless, other attractions, including coastal vegetation, marine life and unique flora and fauna, attract many visitors in equal measure.

USEFUL INFORMATION
MAP REF: C1
Nearest MRT is Kranji. From here it is either SMRT bus 925 to Kranji reservoir carpark and a 15-minute walk, or the Kranji Express bus that goes straight to the Visitor Centre. https://www.sbwr.org.sg/ (C1)

▲ **TOP** The vibrant crimson sunbird is Singapore's unofficial national bird.

▶ **OPPOSITE: CLOCKWISE FROM TOP LEFT** A mangrove crab resting on a tree stump at high tide to keep clear of predators in the tide water.

▶ One of the arboretum shelters on the Mangrove Boardwalk, which can be seen closer up at bottom right.

▶ A bird-watching tower affords wonderful views over lakes, sea and mangroves.

▶ Mangrove forests line Sungei Buloh river at its mouth with views to Johor in Malaysia in the distance. Incidentally, Sungei Buloh translates from the Malay as Bamboo river.

Comprising 130 hectares of mangroves and freshwater wetlands, the park is serviced by a number of trails, ranging in length and location. The 500-metre-long Mangrove Boardwalk gives a good introduction to the shoreline: Equipped with an "outdoor classroom" facility in the form of 20-odd 2-D barcodes that connect to visitors' wireless devices, it is both informative and interesting. Visitors can listen to birdcalls or observe the behaviour of mudskippers through videos streamed over the wireless network. Other longer trails pass through more mud flats, orchards and grassland, as well as now defunct freshwater fishing ponds.

It is estimated that some 140 species of birds regularly pass through the reserve, while many others live here year round. It's also the site for a number of endangered herons' nesting grounds. Between September and April, you'll be able to see many migratory birds, such as plovers and sandpipers, while permanent residents include herons, kingfishers, bitterns, sunbirds and coucals. Monitor lizards, crabs, mudskippers and small fish are also easily spotted.

Many people visit to photograph the pretty crimson sunbird (see top) which appears to favour Sungei Buloh. Like Singapore itself, this bird is often seen as a tiny red dot, flitting from tree to tree with a flash of scarlet. In 2002, it was voted the country's "unofficial national bird" by members of the Singapore Nature Society. Measuring from 10 cm to about 15 cm in length, *Aethopyga sipraja* has a dark crimson back, neck and sides, while the chin and breast are a striking scarlet.

A BEACHFRONT IDYLL FOR WATER SPORTS AND RECREATION

The National Parks' strapline for this 185-hectare park located on the south eastern coast of Singapore—"Recreation for All"—may not be the catchiest, but it does describe the park's key attributes: plenty of sporting, recreational and dining offerings. Boasting a scenic coastline that stretches over 15 km from Changi in the east to Tanjung Rhu near the city centre, the park was opened in the mid 1970s, when the government completed its land reclamation programme off the coast at Katong, and has grown in amenities and facilities ever since.

USEFUL INFORMATION

MAP REF: F3, G3

Many buses run along the East Coast Park Service Road. These include 13, 55 and 155 from Eunos MRT, 31, 196 and 197 from Bedok MRT and 76 and 135 from Paya Lebar MRT. Alternatively, take the underpass from the nearby Marine Parade housing estate, which is served by many public bus routes.

BBQ bookings: http://www.nparks.gov.sg

http://www.manamana.com (G4)

http://www.water-venture.org.sg (G3)

http://www.ski360degree.com/ (G4)

▲ **TOP** A windsurfer takes to the sea. A directional sign showing the way to Ski 360.

◄ **OPPOSITE: CLOCKWISE FROM TOP LEFT** The East Coast Lagoon Food Village is known for its casual outdoor dining.

◄ Many people pitch small tents beneath the sea almond trees lining the ocean, especially if they intend staying for the day.

◄ Rollerblading, wakeboarding, cyling and go-karting are just some of the sports on offer.

The swaying palm trees, casuarinas and sandy beach are alluring enough, but the water, it has to be said, looks a bit murky. If you can get past this, Mana Mana and Water-Venture rent kayaks and windsurfers and a sailing club at the eastern end is well patronized. Land-lubbers can hire bicycles, including tandems, and/or rollerblades, and there's a special track running along the park's perimeter for this purpose.

Those more horizontally inclined can take advantage of a shady spot on (imported) white sand or locally grown grass; barbecue pits are dotted all along and can be booked in advance.

Two more recent additions are Ski 360 and Xtreme Skatepark, both catering mainly to teenagers and manly types in baggy pants or board shorts. The former offers cable-towed wakeboarding or waterskiing in a man-made lagoon set back from the beach. At any one time, eight riders can be on the water simultaneously: depending on ability, there is also a large variety of obstacles such as kickers, a funbox, tabletop, wall rides and so on. It's a fun activity, and the place takes on a party vibe during the evenings.

Local skateboarders have heralded Singapore's first skate park built according to international competition standards with enthusiasm, as it is really far more advanced than any of the city's other designated skating areas. There's a street course section, consisting of obstacles such as stairs, handrails, ledges and gaps, a combo bowl and a vertical bowl, the latter two catering to the more advanced skater/biker. Beautifully built amidst shady parkland, it's a great addition to the city-state. Easy sustenance can be found nearby at the East Coast Lagoon Food Village, a hawker centre that specializes in satay and seafood.

Foodie-wise, the East Coast Seafood Centre, three blocks of casual seafood restaurants, is better known. Here, it's all plastic tables and chairs, jugs of Tiger beer, Singapore-style seafood such as chilli crab and black pepper crab, all with noisy, jostling service and a family-type clientele. There is air-con in some of the restaurants upstairs, but many patrons prefer to eat al fresco to take in both sea views and breezes.

East Coast Park also has bowling alleys, volleyball courts, a mini golf course, tennis and squash courts, as well as holiday chalets if you feel like spending the night. As such, it attracts over 7 million people per year—weekends can get a tad crowded!

THE FLAVOUR OF "OLD SINGAPORE"

Located inland from the East Coast Park is Singapore's eastern suburb of Katong. Traditionally the preserve of the wealthy merchant classes, its heyday was between the wars. Within Katong the area of Joo Chiat is the most interesting: named after landowner and philanthropist Chew Joo Chiat, it was gazetted as a conservation district in 1993.

Today, with nearly 1,000 conservation buildings, a multi-ethnic population and a vibrant living culture, Joo Chiat is like a golden-olden microcosm of the country—a Little Singapore, as it were, without the high-rises. There are mosques, temples, churches and other landmark buildings that reflect Singapore's diversity of culture, rows of beautifully preserved shophouses (and some rather more shambolic ones!), excellent shops and eateries, as well as an all-pervasive "Old Singapore" atmosphere.

Many visit for the Peranakan food: descendants of Chinese immigrants who married local non-Moslems in the Malay archipelago, the Peranakan culture is particularly strong in Joo Chiat. Many of the colourful Rococo-style terrace homes with dashes of chinoiserie in surface decoration (think sculpted façades of animal reliefs and hand-crafted ceramic tiles) were built by middle-class Peranakans between the wars. The rows on Koon Seng Road (see opposite) and Everitt Road are particularly noteworthy. As a result, there are scores of small-scale cafés and restaurants selling the highly individual Peranakan cuisine. Typically blending Chinese ingredients with Malay sauces and spices, it is unique.

Joo Chiat is also famous for its many bakeries specializing in *Nonya kueh* (*Nonyas* are female Peranakans, *kueh* are cakes). Made from a variety of ingredients such as coconut milk, sweet potatoes, tapioca, palm sugar and pandan leaves, they are a speciality of the district. Other foodie delights include *Nonya laksa*, curry puffs, Eurasian and Malay dishes, and more. In fact, everywhere you walk, you'll come across one enticing eatery or another.

Shoppers shouldn't miss the Joo Chiat Complex—more a market, than a shopping centre—with goods as varied as kitchen utensils and crockery, *Nonya*-inspired knick knacks, rare Malay and Indonesian spices, and much more. Also dotted around the area are some smaller boutique-style shops selling antiques, Peranakan arts and crafts, and clothes.

▲ **TOP** The Peranakans are well known for their cuisine: A hearty *laksa*, a coconut curry soup with noodles; a selection of *kueh* or sweets made from glutinous rice, flour, coconut, pandan and herbs, flavoured with *gula Melaka* palm sugar and brightly coloured with natural plant dyes.

▶ **OPPOSITE** Katong's heyday was between the wars, when it was seen as a respectable middle-class neighbourhood. This is verified by its surviving shophouse architecture and the old saying "*gim* Tanglin, *ngeng* Katong" translating as "golden Tanglin, silver Katong". This reflects perfectly the standing in which the two areas were held. Tanglin, with its desirable black-and-white bungalows was a step up from Katong, but the latter with its proximity to the seashore was sought after also.

For the more culturally minded, there's the Sri Senpaga Vinayagar temple in south Indian architectural style; the former Grand Hotel, an impressive Victorian edifice whose gardens were split in two due to the ingress of Still Road (still awaiting re-development); the Church of the Holy Family, a pre-World War II parish church; the Kuan Im Tng temple (Chinese temple of mercy and philanthropy); the serene Masjid Khalid, a compact little mosque; and an interesting exhibition on Eurasian culture at Ceylon Road's Eurasian Community House. Another particularly pleasant aspect of a stroll around Joo Chiat is the opportunity it affords to see age-old crafts in action, such as the crafting of elaborate funerary paraphernalia.

Elsewhere, Katong is mainly residential—blocks of condos lining the East Coast Parkway and rows of terraced houses and bungalows. However, there are a few remaining villas built before and after World War II for the wealthy elite that are worthy of note. In colonial, Eurasian and Peranakan styles, those that have escaped the wrecker's ball are to be found in the Meyer and Mountbatten roads area; before land reclamation they fringed the seashore and were often used as weekend retreats.

USEFUL INFORMATION
MAP REF: F3, F4
Dakota, Paya Lebar, and
Mountbatten MRT stations.
No 16 bus on Joo Chiat Road.
http://www.myjoochiat.com (F4)
http://www.holyfamily.org.sg (F4)
http://www.kuanimtng.org.sg (F4)

◄ **OPPOSITE: CLOCKWISE FROM TOP LEFT** A Peranakan-themed hotel lies behind this pristine white facade in the Joo Chiat area.

◄ Pastel colours, decorative ceramic tiles, Malay-style tracery beneath the roof tiles and Rococo ornamentation were all popular with the Straits Chinese. Tiles on the exterior beneath the windows often featured naturalistic birds and flowers.

◄ Close-up view of a decorative floral tile; often these tiles were fired in relief, as here.

◄ Housed in a traditional shophouse, Rumah Bebe is a treasure trove of Straits Chinese paraphernalia—clothes, bead wares, home-wares and the like.

◄ A selection of pastries and snacks in the dining room at the PeraMakan restaurant.

◄ One of Katong's most famous antique stores is a treasure trove of "old Singapore" items.

◄ *Garam assam* or fish head curry: a delicacy of the area.

Tanjong Katong, Singapore

"THE KING OF KATONG"

The rags-to-riches story of one Chew Joo Chiat had the happy ending that so many 19th-century penniless immigrants dreamt of. Born in 1857 to a peasant family in China's Fujian province, Chew left home at the age of 20 to sail to Singapore to make his fortune. And make his fortune he did.

Aided by hard work and a bit of luck, he worked in a shop and as a ship's chandler, but first made waves as a property developer in the Geylang area, then as a landowner of gambier, nutmeg and pepper. In the early 1900s he bought more land—Confederate estate land and one acre of plantation in today's Joo Chiat area. As people moved eastwards in search of land for housing, Chew bequeathed his Confederate Estate road to the Municipality who promptly paved it opening access to the east. He was then able to cash in on his generosity, by dividing his plantation into building plots for the development of shophouses, terraced houses and bungalows. Thus, the Peranakan and Eurasian enclave of Joo Chiat was born.

By the 1920s, Chew Joo Chiat had become a very prosperous businessman. He had married a Peranakan woman, had children and was now the owner of rubber and coconut plantations in Siglap and Changi. About this time, he turned his hand to banking, founding the Pacific Bank in 1919 and the Batu Pahat bank in Johor a year later. Next came tin mines in the form of the Trengganu and Ulu Pacca Corporations, more rubber and more land.

As was often the case with many early immigrants, Chew never returned to China. He always sent money back "home", he arranged for his children from his first marriage to join him, and he made sure his extended family needed for nothing. A hard grafter, it seems his only recreation came in the form of watching Teochew opera on an opera stage he built across the road from his house. Chew Joo Chiat died on 5th February 1926, and—along with many other early Singapore pioneers—was buried in Bukit Brown Cemetery.

A SOMEWHAT LESS "SQUEAKY CLEAN" SIDE OF TOWN

A paradoxical area, famous for both its brothels and its Buddhist centres, Geylang is the antithesis of straight, squeaky-clean Singapore. It also houses some fantastic local eateries, is one of the best areas in the city-state to buy fresh fruit, and has a wonderful selection of shophouse architecture.

USEFUL INFORMATION
MAP REF: F3, E3, F4
Aljunied, Kallang, Dakota, Mountbatten and Paya Lebar MRT stations.
http://www.thelor24ashophouseseries.com

▲ **TOP** A selection of regional delicacies: Penang *assam laksa*, a sour fish-based noodle dish; *otak otak*, a snack made from fish paste mixed with spices and steamed in a banana leaf; *ayam penyet*, a fried chicken dish, served with *sambal*, *belachan* and *tempe*.

▶ **OPPOSITE TOP** A lively local restaurant spills out onto the sidewalk of a *lorong*. *Kway teow* is a popular regional dish made from flat rice noodles, often accompanied by soy sauce, chilli, a small quantity of *belachan*, whole prawns, deshelled cockles, bean sprouts and chopped Chinese chives. Here, beef is the main attraction.

Located north and south of a 3-kilometre stretch of Geylang Road, along numerous lanes or *lorong* that extend perpendicularly from the main road, Geylang is well worth a visit. It has been spared the gentrification process that has marred other areas in Singapore and retains a vitality that combines with its slightly shambolic air quite nicely.

A lively scene in the form of bars, karaoke lounges, cheap hotels, and a thriving trade in prostitution ensures a hectic nightlife; during the day, things are slightly lower key, but locals often flock to the good hawker-style eateries for lunch and to buy durians in season.

Another draw is the shophouse architecture: Many of the picturesque streets lined with multicoloured shophouses are worth a wander if you're interested in this medium—*lorong* 24A and 34 are a case in point. On one side of 24A, numbers 5, 9, 11, 13, 15, 17, 19 and 21 have been renovated, each by a different architectural practice, to showcase contemporary design within the archetypal shophouse form. You're also likely to hear the sounds of chanting emanating from some interiors; somewhat surprisingly, Geylang is home to a number of Buddhist temples, as well as *dharma* centres, religious schools and martial arts centres.

A little further to the east is Geylang Serai, famous for its wet market and Malay food stalls. Historically, Geylang has been a Malay-dominated area as thousands of Malays and Indonesians moved here from the 1840s onwards to work in the lemongrass (*serai*) plantations and in the copra processing factories. Even though the sad Malay Village, a cultural centre, is an unmitigated disaster, there are plenty of other attractions such as the Geylang Serai Food Centre: with 955 seats above the wet market, it houses a profusion of cheap retail outlets selling batiks and other fabrics, spices, curry powders and the like and a variety of stalls selling Malay and Indian-Muslim specialties. During Ramadan, the food stalls are particularly busy.

芽籠九巷牛河
GEYLANG LOR 9 BEEF KWAY TEOW

嘉坡興安會館三十七年度職員就職典禮留影卅七年元旦

CLAN ASSOCIATIONS

One of the authentic attractions of Geylang is its proliferation of shophouses used by clan associations. Called *huay guan* or "kinship" clubs, these social institutions were the first point of contact for early immigrants. They provided welfare, protection and cultural homogeneity in a land that was full of different nationalities, dialects and cultures. The earliest clan association in Singapore was believed to be the Tsao (or Cao), set up by Tsao Ah Chih, a Cantonese cook who arrived with Raffles. In 1900 there were over 50 clan associations in existence, and, by the 1940s, more than 200. Their role continues today in the form of education, celebration of Chinese festivals, support for the elderly, and as meeting places for their members. An interesting fact is that the famous Chinese painter, Xu Bei Hong, lived for a while in the Nanyang Huang Clan Association in Geylang.

A LAID-BACK VILLAGE ENCLAVE AND A WORLD CLASS AIRPORT

Situated in the northeastern sector of the island, the area of Changi is famous for a number of reasons: It serves as the gateway to the country with its excellent airport, it sports some low-key, picturesque beaches, it is the location of many wartime events and memorials, and it houses the charming hamlet of Changi Village.

Most visitors, however, will get their first sight of Singapore at Changi Airport. It tends to blow most people away, because it is pristine, clean, mind-blowingly efficient and really a pleasant place to pass some time. There are picturesque gardens, spas, hotels, numerous cafés and shops, not to mention free WiFi, a cinema and plenty of lounging space.

In 2012, 51.2 million passengers passed through the airport's hallowed floors. As of January 1, 2013, Changi handled more than 6,500 weekly scheduled flights with 110 airlines connecting Singapore to 240 cities in 60 countries. Its efficiency and amenities clearly contribute to Singapore's appeal as a stopover point for global travellers. Despite the numbers, it never seems crowded and queues are minimal.

Aiming to build on its popular appeal, its budget terminal is currently being demolished to make way for a new facility, Terminal 4. Set to open in 2017, it will be able to handle 16 million more passengers. Now, it has been further announced that a fifth terminal will be added: Codenamed Project Jewel, it will have cutting-edge aviation facilities, as well as extensive retail and recreation outlets. Furthermore, design will be a big factor, as a consortium of design consultants led by world-renowned architect Moshe Safdie, who designed Marina Bay Sands, has been employed to spearhead the project. Watch this space for more news on this exciting development!

If something a little more laid-back is more your style, Changi Village may attract with its low-key appeal. Its charms may not be immediately apparent, but an hour or two in what used to be this quiet little *kampong* will change all that. In the past it was a rubber growing area, but from the 1920s became the colonial government's prime naval base. Military residences still remain today on the hill behind the "village". During the Japanese occupation, it was selected as a POW camp area, and its beach was chosen as one of the mass execution sites for the so-called Sook Ching Operation, where suspected anti-Japanese Chinese civilians were shot. It's estimated that 50,000 such executions took place during the operation. Thankfully, after the war and subsequent independence, the village sank back into its sleepy residential status.

▲ **TOP** Mementoes from the remembrance wall at the Changi Museum: home-made cross-and-poppy token and war medals.

▶ **OPPOSITE: CLOCKWISE FROM TOP LEFT** A pavilion on the Changi Boardwalk mainly used by anglers.

▶ Storyboards at the Changi Museum tell the history of World War II through paintings, photographs and personal effects donated by former POWs.

▶ The boardwalk has views to nearby Pulau Ubin.

▶ Boats lining up at the jetty at Changi Point to take passengers to Pengerang in Johor or to Pulau Ubin.

CHANGI CHAPEL AND MUSEUM

Dedicated to all those who died during World War II especially in the Changi area, this nearby chapel and museum are well worth a visit. The museum displays a collection of wartime memorabilia related to the Japanese occupation, including a remembrance wall that recognizes the various units that defended the country before the Fall; tools, materials and personal belongings of POWs; and storyboards of wartime experiences. You can take an audio tour that includes reminiscences from POWs, locals and war veterans, and take some time for reflection in the somewhat Spartan, open-air courtyard chapel. Built as a representative replica of the many chapels that sprang up during the war, it can provide a moving experience. Like the various holocaust and war museums found all over the globe, this little outpost is also an important educational and resource centre.

Today, the local beach has clean sand, barbecue facilities and fishing areas, but there's not much else to recommend it apart from views to Malaysia and the surrounding islands. It's also the departure point for boats to nearby Pulau Ubin (see overleaf) and forms the beginning of the Eastern Coastal Park Connector, a 42-km route that joins up with the East Coast Park and beyond. This is great for cyclists and runners, and is popular especially at weekends. There's also a 1.2 km boardwalk that snakes around Changi Point giving fine sunset views; it's pleasant for an evening stroll past the sailing club and *kelongs* (fish farms).

The village itself, though modern in construction, is open-air in style, with a number of bars, restaurants and shops. Bargain-hunters will be attracted by the prices—think t-shirts, electronic goods, shoes, batik dresses and the like—but many people come to Changi Village for its superb cuisine. There are plenty of restaurants, bars, coffee shops and cafés, as well as an excellent hawker centre, all serving a wide array of local dishes. Fresh barbecued seafood, *nasi lemak*, fried Hokkien *mee* and many more are all recommended.

Another of Changi Village's attractions is its collection of majestic trees, many of which are over 200 years in age and have a girth of 400 cm or more. As such, it has been designated one of two Tree Conservation Areas in Singapore, a sanctuary for at least 12 very rare and endangered species of native fauna. In addition to some fine Dipterocarps, there are some uncommon coastal trees such as the Sea Trumpet, *chiamau* and *sepetir*, as well as a fine straggling *Ficus stricta*, a rare lowland species.

USEFUL INFORMATION
MAP REF: G2, G3
MRT: Changi Airport
For Changi Village, MRT to Tanah
Merah MRT station, then board bus no
2 to Changi Village bus interchange.

◄ **OPPOSITE: CLOCKWISE FROM TOP LEFT** The exhibition booth at the Singapore Airshow in February 2012 showcases the facilities and design of Changi Airport.

◄ The entrance to Terminal 3 with its unique cantilevered roof form was designed by CPG Consultants.

◄ The arrival sign, in several different languages, at Terminal 2 is surrounded by a plethora of tropical plants and flowers, cementing Singapore's status as a premier Garden City.

◄ The national carrier, Singapore Airlines, is often voted as best airline in international surveys.

◄ Terminal 3 is characterized by patterns and textures in flooring and a roof of layered ceiling panels evoking a rainforest canopy effect.

◄ In addition to the Cactus, Orchid and Enchanted Gardens, there's a Butterfly Garden. Nestled in Terminal 3, it is home to over 1,000 butterflies—a boon for parents with children bored by their long flights.

WHY IS CHANGI AIRPORT CONSISTENTLY RATED THE WORLD'S BEST?

In 2013, Singapore's Changi Airport was once again crowned the best in the world for the fourth time in 14 years at the prestigious World Airport Awards in Geneva. The award was based on surveys conducted by international travel research and consultancy group Skytrax, who polled 12.1 million passengers over a nine-month period. So, why, exactly, is it so popular?

• Not only is the airport efficient, it serves as an entertainment hub. You can spa, swim, drink, eat, go on a nature trail, rest, relax and generally kick back in world-class surrounds.
• Its check-in, arrivals, transfers, shopping, security and immigration facilities are effective in the extreme. Personnel are polite and well-informed and everything works like clockwork.
• The airport offers free city tours to all travellers on a stopover of five hours or more.
• Changi was one of the first airports to introduce free WiFi areas and previously scooped the Skytrax best airport award in 2000 before going on to win again in 2006 and 2010.

SINGAPORE'S LAST FRONTIER

If you've ever wondered what Singapore was like in the 1960s, the rustic, leafy island of Pulau Ubin will give you a pretty good idea. Even though it is part of Singapore, it seems like a completely different time and country. It's Singapore's last wild frontier, you could say.

USEFUL INFORMATION
MAP REF: G2

MRT to Tanah Merah MRT station, then board bus no 2 to Changi Village bus interchange. Take a bumboat from Changi Jetty (now called Changi Point Ferry Terminal), which is near the Changi Village Hawker Centre. NParks Information Kiosk is open 8.30am–5pm. http://www.pulauubin.com.sg/sitemap-navigation.html

▲ **TOP** Some of the wild animals you may chance across: Wild hog smelling a tree trunk; palm civet; lesser mousedeer.

◄ **OPPOSITE: CLOCKWISE FROM TOP LEFT** Fishermen test the waters from a somewhat makeshift jetty.

◄ Palms and bamboos meet above one of the island's rural roads.

◄ A simple Malay-style house on stilts with wooden walls and floors and a corrugated iron roof.

◄ A section of the mangrove-fringed boardwalk at Chek Jawa is a little overgrown.

◄ A secluded cove mainly used by fishermen harks back to an earlier, more simple, time.

Most visitors reach the island from Changi Village on a kerosene belching bumboat that takes 10 to 15 minutes to deposit you at the island's main village. Here you are greeted by *kampong* life in all its glory: About 100 families continue to live on the island in traditional houses without piped water and electricity, relying on farming and fishing for subsistence, while others tend to their provision stores and small restaurants. The rest of the island is covered with dirt paths, bike trails, tidal pools and a wide variety of flora and fauna—including mousedeer, pangolin, palm civets, wild pigs, pythons, at least 180 native and migratory bird species, and over 600 species of plants.

Pulau Ubin, which translates as Granite Island, began to be settled from the mid 19th century onwards. Its undulating, granite hills were viewed as a valuable resource for Singapore's booming construction businesses, and much of the original vegetation was cleared for the cultivation of crops such as rubber, coffee, durian, pineapples and coconuts, amongst others. Today, with many villagers relocated to the mainland, abandoned granite quarries remain as picturesque relics of Ubin's history, while forests and grasslands have regenerated to replace the original primary forest habitats.

Today, the best way to see the island is to hire a bicycle or walk along one of the many nature trails. Most people head to Chek Jawa, a unique nature sanctuary housing a rich coastal and inter-tidal ecosystem. There's a boardwalk from which one can view a vast seagrass lagoon, healthy mangrove swamps, and a diverse shoreline of sandbars, coral rubble and rocks. The visitor centre is housed in a charmingly restored Tudor-style cottage, one of the last remaining in Singapore.

Other highlights on the island include viewing *kampong*-style houses (an old village headman's house is particularly attractive), seafood lunches and cycling or walking in harmony with nature. The diversity of plant and tree life is impressive. This, along with the possibility of bird and animal encounters, makes for an experience that is antithetical to most of the other attractions found in Singapore.

South Singapore

Airports and Access

Singapore's main airport is Changi International Airport, although the smaller Seletar airport receives some flights from nearby destinations.

There are regular ferry services to Changi Point from two destinations in Malaysia, while the Tanah Merah ferry terminal handles ferries from some Indonesian islands.

Access from Malaysia by road occurs at two points: Tuas and Woodlands.

Climate

Singapore is 1 degree north of the equator, so it has a tropical rainforest climate with no distinct seasons. Temperature hovers between a minimum of 23°C and a maximum of 32°C; average annual rainfall is around 2,340 mm (92.1 inches). It is hot, humid and rainy year round.

Currency

Singapore's currency is the Singaporean dollar. One dollar is composed of 100 cents. There are many ATMs around the island and the logos of which cards are accepted at which machine are displayed on the machines.

Banks are usually open from 9.30am to 3pm, Monday through Friday, and are open from 9.30am to 11.30am on Saturdays.

Customs

There is no duty-free concession for cigarettes or other tobacco products. Providing you are not coming from Malaysia, you may bring alcohol up to the following amount: one litre of spirits and one litre of wine; two litres of wine and one litre of beer; one litre of wine and two litres of beer. There are severe penalties for drug trafficking and/or possession.

Electricity

The standard voltage in Singapore is 220V/240V, 50 Hz. If you have equipment that runs on a higher voltage, you should not connect it to Singaporean power unless you have the correct transformer. Singapore uses the British BS1363 three-pronged square pin type socket.

Emergency Telephone Numbers

Ambulance and Fire: 995

Police: 999

Singapore General Hospital: 6222 3322

Getting Around

It is really not worth hiring a car, as Singapore is small, land-locked and all places are easily accessible by bus, MRT (Mass Rapid Transport) and taxi.

Taxis: Taxis are available when the sign on the top of the cab is illuminated and can be hailed on the street. Alternatively, there are numerous taxi ranks around town. Advance bookings and telephone bookings have a booking fee. There is an additional airport surcharge if you take a cab into town from the airport. Comfort/Citycab is the main company; the telephone number is 6552 1111.

There are numerous buses in Singapore under the SBS Transit or SMRT Bus lines. Routes and information can be viewed on www.sbstransit.com.sg and www.smrt.com.sg. Bus service 36 goes to the city from the airport from the basement bus bays of Terminals 1, 2 and 3. The fare is less than S$2 and it takes about an hour.

There is a comprehensive underground/overground train service. For more information and routes, check out the Singapore Mass Rapid Transit website (www.smrt.com.sg).

Mobile Phones

In Singapore, mobile phones operate on GSM900 and GSM1800. Check with your provider if your phone operates on these bands. To avoid high roaming fees, you can buy a local pre-paid SIM card after you arrive.

The international telephone country code for Singapore is 65. To dial overseas, dial 001 before your country code.

Visas

Many nationals are able to visit Singapore for a holiday without a visa, provided they have:

— a valid travel document (minimum validity of 6 months at the time of departure)

— an onward or return ticket (if applicable)

— entry facilities to the next destination

— sufficient funds to stay in Singapore and visa for entry into Singapore (if applicable)

The following countries' people need to apply for a visa:

Afghanistan, Algeria, Bangladesh, Egypt, Georgia, India, Iran, Jordan, Lebanon, Libya, Morocco, Myanmar, Pakistan, People's Republic of China, Holders of Hong Kong Document of Identity, Macau Special Administrative Region Travel Permit, Nigeria, Saudi Arabia, Somalia, Sudan, Syria, Tunisia, Turkmenistan, Ukraine, Yemen, Commonwealth of Independent States (Armenia, Azerbaijan, Belarus, Kazakhstan, Kyrgyzstan, Moldova, Russia, Tajikistan, Uzbekistan), and holders of Palestinian Authority Passport, Temporary Passport issued by the United Arab Emirates and Refugee Travel Document issued by Middle East countries.

Visas may be applied for on-line from:

http://www.mfa.gov.sg/content/mfa/overseasmission/london/visa_information/entryvisa_requirements.html

PHOTO CREDITS